Judith Leyster: A Study of Extraordinary Expression

Nicole Cardinale

2020

i

Contents

List of Illustrations

Fig. 1. Judith Leyster, *Self Portrait*, 1635, oil on canvas, 29 in. x 26 in., National Gallery of Art, Washington.

Fig. 2. Judith Leyster, *Girl with a Straw Hat*, 1635, oil on panel, 14 in. x 12 in., Foundation Rau pour le Tiers-Monde, Zurich.

Fig. 3. Judith Leyster, *A Card Player*, 1630, oil on panel, 13.8 in. x 12.2 in., Private collection.

Fig. 4. Judith Leyster, *Two Children with a Cat*, 1629, oil on canvas, 24 in. x 20 in., Private collection.

Fig. 5. Judith Leyster, *A Boy and a Girl with a Cat and an Eel*, 1630, oil on panel, 23 in. x 19 in., National Gallery, London.

Fig. 6. Attributed to Judith Leyster, *The Jester*, 1625, oil on canvas, 26 in. x 23 in., Rijksmuseum, Amsterdam.

Fig. 7. Frans Hals, *Lute Player*, 1623, oil on canvas, 27 in. x 24 in., Louvre Museum, Paris.

Fig. 8. Abraham Bloemaert, *Shepherd and Shepherdess*, 1627, oil on canvas.

Fig. 9. Adriaen van de Veene, *Bride in Houwelick*, 17th century, etching, University of Amsterdam Library, Netherlands.

Fig. 10. Geertruyd Rogman, *Woman Sewing*, c. 1640-57, engraving, 8 in. x 6 ½ in., The Metropolitan Museum of Art, New York.

Fig. 11. Jan Steen, *In Luxury, Look Out*, 1663, oil on canvas, 40 in. x 57 in., Kunsthistorisches Museum, Vienna.

Fig. 12. Adriaen van Ostade, *Prayer Before the Meal*, 1653, etching, 6 in. x 5 in., British Museum, London.

Fig. 13. Gerrit ter Borch, *Woman Drinking Wine with a Drunken Soldier*, 1658-59, oil on canvas, Private collection.

Fig. 14. Attributed to Cornelis Bisschop, *Self-Portrait of an Artist Seated at an Easel*, c. 1653, oil on panel, 11 in. x 9 in., The Leiden Collection.

Fig. 15. Attributed to Gerrit Dou, *Self-Portrait (?) at an Easel*, c. 1628-29, oil on panel, 26 in. x 20 in., The Leiden Collection.

Fig. 16. Attributed to Gerrit Dou, *Artist at His Easel*, c. 1630-32, oil on panel, 23 ¼ in. x 17 1/8 in., Private collection.

Fig. 17. Rembrandt, *Artist in his Studio*, 1628, oil on panel, Museum of Fine Arts, Boston.

Fig. 18. Pieter Claesz, *Vanitas Still Life*, c. 1628, oil on panel, 14 in. x 23 ½ in., Germanisches Nationalmuseum, Nuremberg.

Fig. 19. Caterina van Hemessen, *Self Portrait*, 1548, oil on panel, 12 in. x 10 in., Öffentliche Kunstsammlungen, Kunstmuseum, Basel.

Fig. 20. Sofonisba Anguissola, *Self Portrait*, 1556, oil on canvas, 26 in. x 22 in., Lancut Museum, Poland.

Fig. 21. Sofonisba Anguissola, *Self Portrait with Bernardino Campi*, 1559, oil on canvas, 43 in. x 39 in., Spannocchi Collection and Pinacoteca Nazionale di Siena, Italy.

Fig. 22. Titian, *Portrait of Clarissa Strozzi*, 1542, oil on canvas, 45 in. x 38 in., Berlin State Museums, Berlin.

Fig. 23. Salomon de Bray, *Shepherdess*, 1635, oil on panel, 8 in. x 6 in., Formerly Robert Noortman Gallery, London.

Fig. 24. Jan Miense Molenaer, *Children Making Music*, c. 1630s, oil on panel, 15.7 in. x 17.5 in., Wawel Castle, Krakow, Poland.

Fig. 25. Sofonisba Anguissola, *Boy Bitten by a Crawfish*, 1554, black chalk and charcoal on brown paper, 13 in. x 15 in., Museo Nazionale di Capodimonte, Naples.

Fig. 26. Eglon Hendrik Van der Neer, *Couple in an Interior*, c. 1675, oil on canvas, 33.6 in. x 27.5 in., Private collection.

Fig. 27. Cornelis Bloemaert, *Child with a Cat*, 1625, engraving, 4 in. x 6 in., Museum of New Zealand, Wellington, New Zealand.

Fig. 28. Jan Steen, *The Effects of Intemperance*, 1663-65, oil on wood, 29 in. x 41 in., National Gallery, London.

Fig. 29. Annibale Carracci, *Two Children Teasing a Cat*, 1590, oil on canvas, 26 in. x 35 in., The Metropolitan Museum of Art, New York.

Fig. 30. Jan Steen, *Children Teaching a Cat to Read*, 1665-68, oil on panel, 17.7 in. x 13.9 in., Kunstmuseum Basel, Switzerland.

Fig. 31. Jan Steen, *Children Teasing a Cat*, 1665, oil on panel, 16 in. x 14 in., Private collection, Kanne, Belgium.

Fig. 32. Jan Steen, *The Cat's Medicine*, 1663, oil on panel, 22 in. x 18 in., San Diego Museum of Art, California.

Fig. 33. Jan Steen, *Children Teaching a Cat to Dance*, 1660-79, oil on panel, 26 in. x 23 in., Rijksmuseum, Amsterdam.

Fig. 34. Judith Leyster, *Self Portrait*, 1653, oil on canvas, 12.1 in. x 8.6 in., Private collection.

Introduction

Depictions of a figure laughing while leaning back in a chair, a girl gazing downward with pensive eyes, and boys conducting mischief through toothy smiles -- few artists depicted such figures more candidly or expressively than Judith Leyster (1609-1660), a phenomenally skillful painter from the so-called Dutch Golden Age.[1] Situated between the career of Sofonisba Anguissola (1535-1625) and Charles Le Brun's *The Expression of the Passions* (1688), Leyster managed to both expand upon earlier explorations of expression and prefigure its codification in the sphere of art production. In the following pages, an in-depth examination of Leyster's use of expression shall be given, whereby her *Self Portrait* (fig. 1) will serve as the ultimate point of reference and provide the framework around which the analysis will focus. Prior to examining her works, a contextual historical stage will be set in which art education and production within the Dutch art market, as well as the hierarchy of genres, will be explicated. Additionally, the traditional uses of expression in early modern portraits and genre scenes will be expounded upon as they relate to Leyster's career. Once contextualized, Leyster's *Self Portrait* will be compared to those by earlier female artists and contemporary male artists to underscore the painting traditions that she wittily re-examined and re-shaped. Then, her *Self Portrait* will be compared to her paintings of children, such as *Girl with a Straw Hat* (fig. 2) and *A Card Player* (fig. 3). Portrayed as spontaneous creatures, the countenances of children permit the greatest scope of natural emotional expression. Hence, by comparing Leyster's *Self Portrait* with these playfully wholesome expressions, the artist's innovative conflation of portraitures and genre

---

[1] Despite the fact that controversy now surrounds the term "Golden Age" due to recent grappling with the legacies of slavery and colonialism, I will use the term throughout this thesis since it is recognized by the art historians who are referenced. On this, see: The New York Times, "A Dutch Golden Age? That's Only Half the Story" https://www.nytimes.com/2019/10/25/arts/design/dutch-golden-age-and-colonialism.html (2-9-20).

scenes will be made all the more apparent. Finally, her paintings of children and animals, including *Two Children with a Cat* (fig. 4) and *A Boy and a Girl with a Cat and an Eel* (fig. 5), will be compared to paintings of children and animals by her contemporaries to emphasize her unique use of expression in perpetuating a certain kind of morality through scenes of mischievous childhood antics while simultaneously preserving their sense of innocence before adulthood. By re-examining portrait traditions, Leyster obscured the line between portraits and genre scenes. Likewise, by capturing fleeting and transient moments of innocent joy, Leyster re-defined what it means to convey expression in painting, expanding its role and tapping into functions that would not become conventional until their codification by Le Brun in the later seventeenth century.

Rather than write about an artist for whom there is an overabundance of written scholarly material, such as Rembrandt or Peter Paul Rubens, to name only two of countless examples, Leyster and the originality of her *Self-Portrait* serve as the starting point for this thesis. The field is not inundated with writings on Leyster, hence allowing an original contribution about her. Drawing on published primary and secondary sources, this book will offer an innovative take on her artworks by underscoring the poised yet playful expressions that punctuated her self-portrait and paintings of children and animals.

The limited scholarly literature on Leyster stems from the fact that she was nearly forgotten about until the late 19th century.[2] As a female painter navigating a patriarchal society, Leyster produced a limited oeuvre that was further restricted upon her marriage to Jan Miense Molenaer (1610-1668), at which point she dedicated herself to advancing his career.[3] In combination with her small oeuvre, she was granted no large commissions; she used only a monogram to sign her works, was not credited in prints made after her pieces, was listed in only

---

[2] Frima Fox Hofrichter, *Judith Leyster: A Woman Painter in Holland's Golden Age* (Doornspijk, Netherlands: Davaco Publishers, 1989), 29.
[3] Frima Fox Hofrichter, *Judith Leyster, 1609–1660* (Washington, DC: National Gallery of Art, 2009), 13.

one known inventory, and received only passing attention during her lifetime for her role as a local curiosity (for being a female painter) rather than for her adroitness as an artist.[4] The reasons for this shall be expounded upon in upcoming chapters.

Alongside her restrictive status as a female artist, Leyster was also largely overlooked because many of her works shared stylistic similarities with and subsequently were misattributed to both her teacher, Frans Hals (1582-1666) and her husband, Molenaer.[5] Bearing in mind the fact that Leyster and Molenaer likely met in Hals's studio, shared the same studio props and models, and needed to create paintings to pay off Molenaer's debts, one could assume that the two artists worked on each other's paintings.[6] This suggestion amounts to mere speculation at best, but nonetheless aids in explaining why the paintings *Youth with a Skull* and *Three Children at a Table*, for example, were alternately ascribed to Leyster and her husband.[7] In regards to misattributions to Hals, a brief comparison between *The Jester* from 1625 (fig. 6), a painting assumed to be by Leyster, and Hals's *Lute Player* from 1623 (fig. 7) will help shed light on why Leyster's paintings were misattributed to the latter artist. At initial glance, the paintings are almost indistinguishable from each other. In both works, the figures are shown in identical half-length poses and against unembellished, neutral-colored backgrounds that ensure viewers focus only on their faces. Accompanied by wide grins, they exaggeratingly cast their animated, roguish eyes upwards towards an unseen light source emanating from the top left corner. This light simultaneously casts stark shadows and illuminates their impish glances and active hands. One can almost hear the strumming of the instruments as the animated hands linger on the strings. Painterly, free-handled brushstrokes compose the compositions, which are further energized by the contrasts between the red and black stripes of the costumes and the pale flesh tones. The stylistic, compositional, and thematic resemblances between these works,

---

[4] Frima Fox Hofrichter, *Judith Leyster: A Woman Painter in Holland's Golden Age* (Doornspijk, Netherlands: Davaco Publishers, 1989), 29.
[5] Ibid, 69.
[6] Ibid, 18.
[7] Ibid, 18, 69.

which are just two of several paintings by Leyster and Hals that are strikingly similar, validate the existence of a professional relationship between the two artists and subsequently render plausible the misattributions of authorship. Whitney Chadwick has also proposed that, in conjunction with these stylistic similarities and professional relationship as master and pupil, Leyster's "inferior" status as a female painter may explain the misidentification by previous generations of scholars of her works to other male artists.[8] From this, I postulate that closely tied historical and stylistic factors contributed to her being forgotten. This thesis aspires to dispel those factors by focusing not on Leyster's gender, but rather on her passion for cultivating expression to merge conventional painting genres.

LITERATURE REVIEW

Most misattributions were made during the eighteenth century, with the exception of *Two Children with a Cat*, which was misidentified in the seventeenth century by Justus Danckerts, an art dealer, publisher, and engraver working primarily in Amsterdam.[9] He labeled the work as a Hals due to his unfamiliarity with Leyster's monogram signature (an entwined "J" and "L" with a shooting star), and also due to the fact that the work was sold as a workshop piece when Leyster presumably painted under Hals's direction.[10] Due to other misinterpretations of her monogram, Leyster's *The Happy Couple* from 1630, as well as her *Portrait of a Woman* from 1635, were similarly assigned to Hals.[11] The latter work was assumed by German art historian and curator, Wilhelm von Bode, to be by an individual named Jan Hals because of the

---

[8] Whitney Chadwick, *Women, Art and Society* (London: Thames & Hudson, 1990), 24. For further study, see Rozsika Parker and Griselda Pollock, *Old Mistresses: Women, Art, and Ideology* (New York: Pantheon Books, 1981).
[9] Frima Fox Hofrichter, *Judith Leyster: A Woman Painter in Holland's Golden Age* (Doornspijk, Netherlands: Davaco Publishers, 1989), 45.
[10] Ibid.
[11] Ibid, 61.

prominence of the "J."[12] Likewise, Leyster's *Carousing Couple* from 1630 was incorrectly

ascribed to Hals in 1758 due to Austro-Hungarian psychologist Max Wertheimer's postulation

that the monogram on the work was somehow an amalgamation of all of the letters of Hals's

name.[13] The painting was not correctly attributed to Leyster until 1892, when Lawrie & Co., a

former London art dealership and gallery, filed suit against Wertheimer for misrepresenting the

work as a Hals.[14] Consequently, the court reduced the fiscal value of the work and concluded

that the mistaken attribution to Hals was made without malicious intent.[15]

The rest of the misattributed works were correctly ascribed to Leyster in 1893, when

Dutch art collector, art historian, and museum curator, Cornelis Hofstede de Groot, realized the

error made by Danckerts, Bode, and Wertheimer, and that the monogram actually belonged to

Leyster due to the presence of the star symbol, which was a reference to the surname Leyster, or

lodestar, meaning "comet" in Dutch.[16] Among the first academically-trained art historians of the

Netherlands, de Groot published his realization as an addendum to a short article on Leyster in

the journal *Jahrbuch der Königlich Preussischen Kunstsammlungen* (*Yearbook of the Royal

Prussian Art Collections*) in 1893.[17]

De Groot's reattribution of *The Happy Couple* to Leyster in 1893 and subsequent journal

article catalyzed a renewed interest in her work.[18] The battle, however, was far from being won.

In 1918, Frieda van Emden published a short notice in which Leyster was referred reductively to

as a "female Frans Hals."[19] In 1927, Juliane Harms provided the first extended study of Leyster

---

[12] Ibid.
[13] Ibid, 46.
[14] Ibid.
[15] Ibid.
[16] Cornelis Hofstede de Groot, "Judith Leyster. Mit einer Lichtdrucktafel und zwei Abbildungen im Text," *Jahrbuch der Königlich Preussischen Kunstsammlungen* 14 (1893): 190-198, 232.
[17] Ibid.
[18] Ann Sutherland Harris and Linda Nochlin, *Women Artists: 1550-1950* (Los Angeles: Museum Associates of the Los Angeles County Museum of Art, 1976), 137.
[19] Frieda van Emden, "Judith Leyster, a Female Frans Hals," *The Art World* 3 (March, 1918): 502.

when she published her doctoral dissertation, titled *Judith Leyster: ihr Leben und ihr Werk*.[20] It was not until the 1970s, however, with the emergence of the women's movement, on the one hand, and a renewed interest in Hals, on the other, that Leyster was regularly included in surveys of women artists written by Linda Nochlin and Ann Sutherland Harris, among numerous others.[21] Much more substantial consideration was given to Leyster when Frima Fox Hofrichter published her PhD dissertation on Leyster as a book in 1989.[22] Since then, a plethora of other art historians, including Elizabeth Alice Honig, James Welu, Pieter Biesboer, Jakob Rosenberg, and Simon Schama, among many others, have, and continue, to enrich our understanding of Leyster's life and career via their comprehensive research and writings.[23]

Of the aforementioned scholars, Welu and Biesboer have published what is arguably the most comprehensive study of Leyster, titled *Judith Leyster: A Dutch Master and Her World* (1993). This detailed book accompanied the first ever museum exhibition dedicated to Leyster's oeuvre in 1993, which marked the one-hundredth anniversary of her rediscovery and traveled from her native Haarlem to the Worcester Art Museum in Worcester, Massachusetts, where it was displayed from September 19th to December 5th of that year.[24]

Finally, in recent times, a 2009 exhibition at the National Gallery of Art in Washington, D.C. commemorating the 400th anniversary of Leyster's birth provided the artist's second but

---

[20] Juliane Harms, "Judith Leyster, ihr Leben und ihr Werk," *Oud-Holland* 44 (1927).
[21] Frima Fox Hofrichter, *Judith Leyster: A Woman Painter in Holland's Golden Age* (Doornspijk, Netherlands: Davaco Publishers, 1989), 33; Linda Nochlin, "Why Have There Been No Great Women Artists?" from *Art and Sexual Politics* (London: Collier Macmillan, 1973); Ann Sutherland Harris and Linda Nochlin, *Women Artists: 1550-1950* (Los Angeles: Museum Associates of the Los Angeles County Museum of Art, 1976).
[22] Frima Fox Hofrichter, *Judith Leyster: A Woman Painter in Holland's Golden Age* (Doornspijk, Netherlands: Davaco Publishers, 1989).
[23] Elizabeth Alice Honig, "The Art of Being 'Artistic': Dutch Women's Creative Practices in the 17th Century," *Woman's Art Journal* 22 (2001-2002); James A. Welu and Pieter Biesboer, *Judith Leyster: A Dutch Master and Her World* (Worcester: Waanders Printers, Zwolle, 1993); Jakob Rosenberg et al., *The Pelican History of Art: Dutch Art and Architecture 1600-1800* (Baltimore, Maryland: Penguin Books Inc., 1972); Simon Schama, "Wives and Wantons: Versions of Womanhood in 17th Century Dutch Art," *The Oxford Art Journal* 3 (1980).
[24] Worcester Art Museum, *Judith Leyster: A Dutch Master and Her World* (Worcester, Massachusetts: Worcester Art Museum, 1993), 1. Exhibition pamphlet.

most substantial retrospective in the United States.[25] The exhibition featured ten of Leyster's works and fifteen by her contemporaries, including Hals and Molenaer, and had a companion show at the Frans Hals Museum in Haarlem. A third show featuring her work recently concluded at the National Museum of Women in the Arts in Washington, D.C., titled *Women Artists of the Dutch Golden Age*. The show, which ran from October 11, 2019 to January 5, 2020, was the first of its kind to explore the contributions of women artists during the Dutch Golden Age and included pieces by Leyster, Maria Sibylla Merian (1647-1717), Magdalena van de Passe (1600-1638), Clara Peeters (born 1594), Rachel Ruysch (1664-1750), Maria Schalcken (1645-1699), Anna Maria van Schurman (1607-1678) and Alida Withoos (1661-1730).[26]

Catalogues for these exhibitions and works by the above scholars shall be incorporated as secondary sources in this study to provide intrinsic economic, socio-political, and artistic contexts surrounding Leyster's career. Primary-source voices will include those of Baldassare Castiglione (1478-1529), Pomponius Gauricus (1482-1530), Giorgio Vasari (1511-1574), Samuel Ampzing (1590-1632), Jacob Cats (1577-1660), René Descartes (1596-1650), Charles Le Brun (1619-1690), and Johan van Nyenborch (1621-1670). Upon initial glance, Castiglione and Vasari, both of whom were Italian Renaissance authors, may seem incongruous with a study pertaining to seventeenth-century Holland. However, Castiglione's description of the ideal woman and the virtues she should possess, as well as Vasari's words of praise for Sofonisba Anguissola, are exemplified in discursive framing of Leyster and her works. Likewise, the inclusion of Lavinia Fontana (1552-1614), a Bolognese Mannerist painter, and Catharina van Hemessen (1528-1588), a Flemish Renaissance painter, may seem impertinent at first glance. A brief delineation of their careers, though, aid in highlighting the patriarchal circumstances to which and with which Leyster and her female contemporaries and predecessors dealt and responded. How Leyster chose to respond to them is perceptible in her works, as shall be outlined in upcoming chapters.

---

25 Frima Fox Hofrichter, *Judith Leyster, 1609–1660* (Washington, DC: National Gallery of Art, 2009), 1.
26 National Museum of Women in the Arts, *Women Artists of the Dutch Golden Age* (Washington, D.C.: National Museum of Women in the Arts, 2019), 1. Exhibition pamphlet.

In Chapter 1, I will provide a historical context and an overview of the uses of expression in early modern portraiture and genre scenes in order to provide a better understanding of the circumstances with which Leyster had to contend. Such circumstances included the training of primarily male apprentices in the Dutch art market, the hierarchy of genres, how the further specialization of different genres corresponded with an influx of customers across all social strata, the spirit of independence that the formation of the Dutch Republic generated, the domestic portrayals of women in genre scenes, and Le Brun's later codification of expression in the academic context. In Chapter 2, I will compare Leyster's self-portrait to those of her male contemporaries, such as Cornelis Bisschop (1630-1674), Gerrit Dou (1613-1675), Rembrandt van Rijn (1606-1669), and Pieter Claesz (1597-1661), and female predecessors, including Caterina van Hemessen and Sofonisba Anguissola, in order to argue that Leyster's use of expression differed from even the most pioneering of self-portraits. Chapter 3 compares Leyster's self-portrait with her own paintings of children in order to show that these works not only blend portraits and genre scenes, but also waver between childlike innocence and mature, adult poses. Chapter 4 compares Leyster's paintings of children and animals to those of her contemporaries, thereby showing that the ability of her imagery to vacillate between infancy and adulthood separated her works from those of her peers. In the final analysis, this book endeavors to examine Leyster through a fresh perspective. Rather than focus on her as a "female Frans Hals" or a female artist in general, the following chapters consider her an artist deeply interested in the exploration of expression in art and in blending conventional categories, such as portraiture and genre scenes, in painting.

Chapter 1: Historical Context and the Uses of Expression in Portraiture and Genre Scenes

The eighth child of Jan Willemsz, a cloth-maker who operated a brewery called Ley/sterre, or Lodestar, Judith Leyster was a notable genre painter from Haarlem who simultaneously continued and re-examined the Dutch painting tradition during Holland's Golden Age.[27] By age nineteen, she had already been listed and applauded by seventeenth-century historian and art lover Samuel Ampzing in his *Description and Praise of the City of Haarlem in Holland* from 1628 as an artist of "good and keen insight" working in Haarlem.[28] His praise accompanied the rhetorical question, "Who has ever seen paintings by a daughter?" in reference to that fact that being a female painter was extraordinarily rare; moreover, she was not trained by her father as was the tradition.[29] Ampzing's mentioning of Leyster was particularly perceptive, for her career became firmly established in the 1630s.[30] More significantly, Leyster became the first of only two women (the other being Sara van Baalbergen [1607-1638]) for whom works are documented to be accepted as a member of the Saint Luke's Guild of Haarlem in the seventeenth century.[31] The period during which the guild was founded

---

[27] Frima Fox Hofrichter, *Judith Leyster: A Woman Painter in Holland's Golden Age* (Doornspijk, Netherlands: Davaco Publishers, 1989), 13; Jakob Rosenberg, et al., *The Pelican History of Art: Dutch Art and Architecture 1600-1800* (Baltimore, Maryland: Penguin Books Inc., 1972), 176; Ann Sutherland Harris, *Seventeenth-Century Art & Architecture* (Upper Saddle River, New Jersey: Pearson Education, Inc., 2005), 358.
[28] Samuel Ampzing, *Beschrijvinge ende Lof der stad Haelem in Holland* (Haarlem: Adriaen Rooman, 1628) quoted in University of Maryland's *Early Modern Women* (College Park, Maryland: Center for Renaissance & Baroque Studies, University of Maryland, 2010), 261.
[29] Samuel Ampzing, *Beschrijvinge ende Lof der stad Haelem in Holland* (Haarlem: Adriaen Rooman, 1628) quoted in Institute for Art Historical Research's *Artibus et Historiae: An Art Anthology* (Cracow, Poland: IRSA, 2008), 9-10.
[30] Frima Fox Hofrichter, *Judith Leyster, 1609–1660* (Washington, DC: National Gallery of Art, 2009), 1.
[31] Wayne E. Franits, *Dutch Seventeenth-Century Genre Painting: Its Stylistic and Thematic Evolution* (New Haven and London: Yale University Press, 2004), 48. Named after the Evangelist Luke, patron saint of artists, the Guild of Saint Luke formed following the reinstatement of trade between the Spanish Netherlands and the Dutch Republic with the Twelve Years' Truce in 1609. On this, see: Stephan R. Epstein and Maarten Roy Prak, *Guilds, Innovation and the European Economy, 1400–1800* (Cambridge: Cambridge University Press, 2008), 151-2; Randall Lesaffer, *The Twelve Years Truce (1609): Peace,*

saw an increase in immigration, which led to the need for many Dutch cities to establish protection against the great number of paintings that began to cross the border.[32] The guild, however, was highly inclusive of artistic practice and identity, representing everyone from painters, sculptors, and other visual artists to dealers, amateurs, and connoisseurs.[33]

Manager of her own workshop, Leyster competed with the likes of her former master, Hals, and even took on male pupils.[34] In 1635, a lawsuit between Leyster and Hals, whereby Leyster won a settlement for the unlawful acceptance of one of her pupils in Hal's studio, further confirms her professional status as a worthy competitor.[35] She produced only a small body of work that ceased almost entirely upon her marriage in 1636 to Molenaer, whom, as has been stated, she met in Hal's studio where they were both students. From that point on, she helped him sell his works. Despite her small oeuvre, Leyster is nevertheless worthy of an analysis equal to that of her better-known contemporaries.[36]

THE DUTCH ART MARKET

Understanding the production practices that comprised the Dutch art market within which Leyster painted will aid in framing this analysis. Accordingly, the rest of this chapter will

Truce, War and Law in the Low Countries at the Turn of the 17th Century (Leiden: Martinus Nijhoff Publishers, 2014), 1.

[32] Maarten Roy Prak, *Craft Guilds in the Early Modern Low Countries: Work, Power and Representation* (Farnham, UK: Ashgate Publishing, 2006), 241.

[33] Ibid, 249.

[34] Jakob Rosenberg, et al., *The Pelican History of Art: Dutch Art and Architecture 1600-1800* (Baltimore, Maryland: Penguin Books Inc., 1972), 176; James A. Welu and Pieter Biesboer, *Judith Leyster: A Dutch Master and Her World* (Worcester: Waanders Printers, Zwolle, 1993), 12; Elizabeth Alice Honig, "The Art of Being 'Artistic': Dutch Women's Creative Practices in the 17th Century," *Woman's Art Journal* 22 (2001-2002): 31.

[35] Frima Fox Hofrichter, *Judith Leyster: A Woman Painter in Holland's Golden Age* (Doornspijk, Netherlands: Davaco Publishers, 1989), 15-16.

[36] James A. Welu and Pieter Biesboer, *Judith Leyster: A Dutch Master and Her World* (Worcester: Waanders Printers, Zwolle, 1993), 13; Horace Shipp, *The Dutch Masters* (New York: Philosophical Library, Inc., 1953), 65; Elsa Honig Fine, "One Point Perspective," *Woman's Art Journal* 16 (1995-1996): 2.

be devoted to describing the art market conditions that were specific to the seventeenth-century Dutch Republic during Leyster's career. According to Neil de Marchi and Hans van Miegroet, paintings that generate the greatest viewing pleasure are those that balance visual challenge with pleasing aesthetics.[37] Variety and invention are the keys to sustaining this balance.[38] The theory I will put forth is that Leyster's paintings contain a degree of multiplicity and ingenuity that was unmatched by her predecessors and contemporaries.

In the Dutch Republic, the production and marketing of images prospered within guild organizations, which were associations of skilled workers who supervised the executions of their crafts or trades in particular fields.[39] Artists had already been organized in guilds since the late Middle Ages.[40] Yet as the Dutch art market expanded in the early seventeenth century, autonomous guilds dedicated solely to the visual arts were founded.[41] These newly-developed Dutch artist guilds reflected the refinement of expertise in many industries as well as a burgeoning realization among painters and printmakers as to the desirability and prestige of their skills.[42] As a result, these guilds lent the fine arts an elevated status and aided in properly training young artists to participate in the making and marketing of paintings.[43]

Before becoming painters and printmakers and joining guilds, teenage boys would complete apprenticeships under the guidance and instruction of master artists.[44] Girls seldom followed the same procedures, thus making Leyster's training and subsequent management of a studio exceedingly rare.[45] Occupation options open to educated, literate women of the middle and upper classes such as Leyster were limited to attending dame schools (small private schools

37 Ibid.
38 Ibid.
39 Claartje Rasterhoff, "Economic Aspects of Dutch Art" in Wayne E. Franits' *The Ashgate Research Companion to Dutch Art of the Seventeenth Century* (New York: Routledge, 2016), 364.
40 Ibid.
41 Ibid.
42 Ibid.
43 Ibid.
44 Patrick Wallis, *Apprenticeship in Early Modern Europe* (Cambridge, UK: Cambridge University Press, 2019), 309, 312.
45 Ibid, 141, 310.

operated by women), taking private lessons, self-teaching through books, or pursuing artistic endeavors such as writing, drawing, or painting, so long as they remained hobbies.[46] The restriction of artistic pursuits to mere hobbies may be explained by the fact that women artists were automatically deemed "amateurs" or "craftswomen," and therefore not in need of upper-level training outside the confines of the home.[47] Secondly, the capacity for women to study the male nude, go on unaccompanied sketching trips to Rome in order to study ancient sculpture, and collect the raw resources that grand genres such as history painting necessitated, was unheard of and regarded as indecent.[48]

Apprentices, while residing as boarders under the masters' roofs, began by learning the basics of maintaining studios, which included prepping and priming canvases and panels, readying drawings for transfer, grinding pigments, and mixing pigments with oils.[49] After grasping the basics of studio maintenance, apprentices learned to draw by observing their masters' works, studying antique statues, and recording the anatomy of models.[50] Since it was unsuitable for female apprentices, however, to draw naked bodies from life, they studied anatomy by examining sculpture and sometimes by using members of their households as models (as Anguissola, for example, was instructed to do), though these male figures were always clothed.[51] Occasional drawings of nudes were practiced in loosely-formed academies that existed in conjunction with guilds, but women, as Linda Nochlin pointed out, were denied access to this crucial aspect of a "great" artist's training.[52] Upon conquering fundamental drawing

[46] Rudolf Michel Dekker, "Women in the Medieval and Early Modern Netherlands," *Journal of Women's History* 10.2 (1998): 174-175.
[47] Elizabeth Alice Honig, "The Art of Being 'Artistic': Dutch Women's Creative Practices in the 17th Century," *Woman's Art Journal* 22 (2001-2002): 31.
[48] Linda Nochlin, "Why Have There Been No Great Women Artists?" from *Art and Sexual Politics* (London: Collier Macmillan, 1973), 24-5; Ann Sutherland Harris and Linda Nochlin, *Women Artists: 1550-1950* (Los Angeles: Museum Associates of the Los Angeles County Museum of Art, 1976), 29.
[49] Caroline P. Murphy, *Lavinia Fontana: A Painter and her Patrons in Sixteenth-century Bologna* (New Haven and London: Yale University Press, 2003), 21.
[50] Ibid.
[51] Ibid, 21-22; Leticia Ruiz Gómez, *A Tale of Two Women Painters: Sofonisba Anguissola and Lavinia Fontana* (Madrid: Museo Nacional del Prado, 2019), 89.
[52] Linda Nochlin, "Why Have There Been No Great Women Artists?" from *Art and Sexual Politics* (London: Collier Macmillan, 1973), 24.

techniques, apprentices were taught to paint, first by copying their masters' works and later by contributing minor parts to them, such as the costumes and landscape background features.[53] Regardless of how little or how much apprentices contributed to their masters' paintings, masters typically sold these collaborative pieces solely under their names.[54] Pupils rarely had the chance to do the same.[55] Two to four years into apprenticeships, students were expected to pass a test which consisted of painting a masterpiece that was retained by the guild and demonstrated the honing of their skills.[56] Leyster's *Self Portrait*, for example, upon its completion in 1633, was offered as a masterpiece to the Haarlem Guild of Saint Luke.[57] Due to the lack of sufficient funding, only a minor number of apprentices who passed the test went on to open their own studios and adopt pupils.[58] More typically, apprentices who passed the test continued on as journeymen or laborers in the studios in which they trained.[59] Since painters' professions ranged from apprentices and journeymen to autonomous masters, court officials, and affluent artists who painted as a hobby, their social statuses spanned all classes.[60] Despite the fact that the majority of master painters were men, some female artists achieved this status by painting for pleasure.[61] In seventeenth-century Holland, more than a dozen women (Sara van Baalbergen possibly among them) were documented as having acquired the title of Master, Leyster being the most renowned of them.[62]

---

[53] Mariet Westermann, *A Worldly Art: The Dutch Republic, 1585-1718* (New York: Harry N. Abrams, Incorporated, 1996), 31.
[54] Ibid.
[55] Ibid.
[56] Maarten Roy Prak, *Craft Guilds in the Early Modern Low Countries: Work, Power and Representation* (Farnham, UK: Ashgate Publishing, 2006), 241.
[57] Frima Fox Hofrichter, *Judith Leyster, 1609–1660* (Washington, DC: National Gallery of Art, 2009), 7.
[58] Patrick Wallis, *Apprenticeship in Early Modern Europe* (Cambridge, UK: Cambridge University Press, 2019), 313.
[59] Ibid.
[60] Mariet Westermann, *A Worldly Art: The Dutch Republic, 1585-1718* (New York: Harry N. Abrams, Incorporated, 1996), 31.
[61] Ibid, 32.
[62] Ibid.

A wide range of income levels and social statuses comprised not only those in the painting profession, but also those who bought and collected the works produced by them.[63] Despite the complete lack of official church patronage due to Calvinism, which forbade the use of altarpieces, any representation of God or Christ, and the idolization of saints, the Dutch Republic flourished following the Treaty of Antwerp in 1609 (a termination of conflict between the Habsburg rulers of Spain and the Southern Netherlands and the Dutch Republic).[64] This period of peace allowed for many private individuals to become ardent collectors of art.[65] While some were peasants or laborers who could afford to purchase a few ordinary prints at most, the majority were burghers (middle-class citizens), a class which ranged from the humblest of artisans to well-to-do regents.[66] In 1648, the Netherlands and Spain agreed to peaceful relations following the Treaty of Münster, thus ushering in a thriving economy.[67] With the boom came a wealthier middle class that purchased more and larger paintings to decorate each room of their inns, shops, and houses.[68]

This endeavor to decorate one's house during a time of economic prosperity in the seventeenth century closely resembles the accumulation of art and decoration of houses in Antwerp in the mid-sixteenth century, as the standard of living improved for the middle class and the general population increased.[69] According to a study by Maximiliaan P.J. Martens and Natasja Peeters of inventories of confiscated goods from between 1532 and 1567, the increased possession of pictures among the middle class may be attributed to the higher classes shifting

[63] Frima Fox Hofrichter, *Judith Leyster, 1609–1660* (Washington, DC: National Gallery of Art, 2009), 7.
[64] Jonathan Israel, *The Dutch Republic: Its Rise, Greatness, and Fall, 1477–1806* (Oxford: Clarendon Press, 1995), 404-406, 410; Claartje Rasterhoff, "Economic Aspects of Dutch Art" in Wayne E. Franits' *The Ashgate Research Companion to Dutch Art of the Seventeenth Century* (New York: Routledge, 2016), 361-62.
[65] Steven Felix-Jäger and Amos Yong, *Pentecostal Aesthetics: Theological Reflections in a Pentecostal Philosophy of Art and Aesthetics* (Boston: Brill Academic Publishers, 2015), 22.
[66] Mariet Westermann, *A Worldly Art: The Dutch Republic, 1585-1718* (New York: Harry N. Abrams, Incorporated, 1996), 33.
[67] Jonathan Israel, *The Dutch Republic: Its Rise, Greatness, and Fall, 1477–1806* (Oxford: Clarendon Press, 1995), 596-597.
[68] Frima Fox Hofrichter, *Judith Leyster, 1609–1660* (Washington, DC: National Gallery of Art, 2009), 7.
[69] Neil De Marchi, and Hans J. Van Miegroet, *Mapping Markets for Paintings in Europe, 1450-1750.* (Turnhout, Belgium: Brepols Publishers, 2006), 37, 39.

their focus from paintings made readily available by economic prosperity to paintings of extraordinary brilliance, therefore leading to the formations of the first large private collections of paintings in the mid-sixteenth century.[70] An additional explanation for middle class ownership may have been their desire to emulate the elite (a desire that they were able to fulfill owing to artists' adoptions of lower-cost production methods that rendered paintings attainable).[71] These prestigious collections, as well as the more modest ones of the middle class, adorned the homes of their respective owners. The inventories from these homes show that the number of art objects in each collection (primarily paintings) directly correlated with the sizes of the houses.[72] Approximately half of the artworks were kept and displayed in the downstairs levels, while the rest were unequally dispersed amongst the other rooms, especially the primary upstairs bedrooms, mezzanines, and kitchens.[73] Panel paintings were the chief art objects to adorn the walls of the downstairs rooms, likely because these were areas where guests were welcomed.[74] Of the religious, mythological, and allegorical subjects on display, those that alluded to antique and contemporary Italian and French Renaissance culture were most popular.[75] In terms of secular images, portraits dominated, while landscapes and genre scenes were found among all classes but in low numbers.[76] The Dutch mirrored these socio-economic conditions and middle and upper class collecting habits moving into the seventeenth-century.[77]

Only one inventory list from February 26, 1669 that belonged to Gerrit ten Bergh, Leyster's brother-in-law located in Haarlem, is known to have contained any of Leyster's works

---

[70] Ibid, 43.
[71] Ibid, 50.
[72] Ibid.
[73] Ibid.
[74] Ibid.
[75] Ibid.
[76] Ibid, 51.
[77] Neil De Marchi, and Hans J. Van Miegroet, *Mapping Markets for Paintings in Europe, 1450-1750* (Turnhout, Belgium: Brepols Publishers, 2006), 35.

(more precisely, two unnamed, low-value comical paintings that hung in his kitchen).[78] Despite Leyster's scant documented presence in private collections, a discussion of seventeenth-century art collectors is nevertheless pertinent here.

Herman Becker (1617-1678), a wealthy Amsterdam ship freighter and moneylender, serves as an ideal example of an affluent seventeenth-century Dutch art collector who was acquiring works at the time of Leyster's career.[79] The inventory of Becker's collection upon his death in 1678 lists works spanning a vast range of subjects, styles, artists, and dates, including paintings by Pieter Bruegel the Elder (1525-1569), Adriaen Brouwer (1605-1638), Gerard ter Borch (1617-1681), Jan Steen (1626-1679), and Gabriel Metsu (1629-1677).[80] Unattributed genre scenes in Becker's collection contained a multitude of subject matters, including images of peasant life.[81] By amassing such a versatile collection, Becker demonstrated the fact that the tastes of many wealthy Dutch collectors transcended the elitist endeavor to maintain a poised façade of only "noble" subjects, thereby predicting the increased development of different genres in the seventeenth and eighteenth centuries.[82]

The further specialization of different genres corresponded with an influx of customers across all social strata.[83] Portraits in particular were purchased by people of every social standing, including merchants, artisans, and militiamen.[84] Aristocrats, magistrates, and wealthy merchants, especially in the 1620s and 1630s, popularized a type of portrait and history painting known as the pastoral scene, or depictions of shepherds and shepherdesses inhabiting plush,

---

[78] Pieter Biesboer, *Collections of Paintings in Haarlem 1572-1745* (Los Angeles: J. Paul Getty Museum, 2002), 213; Dennis P. Weller, *Jan Miense Molenaer: Painter of the Dutch Golden Age* (Manchester, VT: Hudson Hills, 2002), 60.
[79] Linda Stone-Ferrier, "An Assessment of Recent Scholarship on Seventeenth-Century Dutch Genre Imagery" in Wayne E. Franits' *The Ashgate Research Companion to Dutch Art of the Seventeenth Century* (New York: Routledge, 2016), 83.
[80] Ibid, 84.
[81] Ibid.
[82] Ibid, 83.
[83] Frima Fox Hofrichter, *Judith Leyster, 1609–1660* (Washington, DC: National Gallery of Art, 2009), 7.
[84] Mariet Westermann, A Worldly Art: The Dutch Republic, 2585-1718 (New York: Harry N. Abrams, Incorporated, 1996), 40.

scenic landscapes.[85] An excellent example is Abraham Bloemaert's *Shepherd and Shepherdess* from 1627 (fig. 8). Situated before a low horizon line and framed by sheep and a tree with overhanging branches, a shepherd and shepherdess are shown resting on a grassy knoll, taking a respite from the growing urbanization of the period. Since pastoral scenes came to be associated with aristocrats by the mid-seventeenth century, burghers endeavoring to elevate their status began purchasing these works as well.[86] Even iconoclastic Calvinists participated in the art market by purchasing pastoral paintings as a way of drawing parallels with the biblical Garden of Eden, and images of Old Testament scenes as a form of biblical instruction.[87] Furthermore, collectors purchased art for more than mere aesthetic, decorative, or status-raising purposes. Rather, they also acquired art for the sake of interpreting and engaging with various issues and forms of knowledge.[88]

Inevitably, in an attempt to cater to particular markets and demographics, namely burghers and aristocrats, painters altered their techniques and styles.[89] Modulating elements of personal style to be represented in the collections of the rich and powerful was considered a worthwhile endeavor.[90] If held in high regard by influential clients and merchants, artists could publicize these connections and acquire fame, which would then lead to higher prices for their paintings.[91] The benefits of this process were therefore lucrative and crucial for building artistic

---

[85] Alan R. Ruff, *Arcadian Visions: Pastoral Influences on Poetry, Painting and the Design of Landscape* (Oxford, UK: Windgather Press, 2015), 56.
[86] Linda Stone-Ferrier, "An Assessment of Recent Scholarship on Seventeenth-Century Dutch Genre Imagery" in Wayne E. Franits' *The Ashgate Research Companion to Dutch Art of the Seventeenth Century* (New York: Routledge, 2016), 83.
[87] Steven Felix-Jäger and Amos Yong, *Pentecostal Aesthetics: Theological Reflections in a Pentecostal Philosophy of Art and Aesthetics* (Boston: Brill Academic Publishers, 2015), 22; Alan R. Ruff, *Arcadian Visions: Pastoral Influences on Poetry, Painting and the Design of Landscape* (Oxford, UK: Windgather Press, 2015), 55.
[88] Linda Stone-Ferrier, "An Assessment of Recent Scholarship on Seventeenth-Century Dutch Genre Imagery" in Wayne E. Franits' *The Ashgate Research Companion to Dutch Art of the Seventeenth Century* (New York: Routledge, 2016), 83.
[89] Frima Fox Hofrichter, *Judith Leyster, 1609–1660* (Washington, DC: National Gallery of Art, 2009), 7.
[90] M.E.W. Boers, "Pieter De Molijn (1597-1661): A Dutch Painter and the Art Market in the Seventeenth Century," *Journal of Historians of Netherlandish Art* (2017): 8.
[91] Ibid.

reputations.[92] To produce works that would attract wealthy collectors and fetch higher prices at market, some artists spent lengthier-than-average periods of time creating works that were decisively more extravagant and refined than usual.[93] For instance, artists began expanding their use of larger canvases to accommodate the requests of the upper-middle class for larger paintings.[94] Additionally, some landscape painters selling on the open market shifted between executing polished works dotted with figures and making schematic landscapes with swift brushwork, thin layers of paint, and fewer figures.[95] The latter type required less time, less money, and fewer materials, and could therefore be produced in larger quantities to sell.[96] Though these works did not fetch high prices at market, they had the potential to sell quickly, thus making up for the smaller profits and permitting art to be within reach of even the most unassuming townsmen.[97]

Painters not only altered their personal styles so as to cater to certain classes, but also chose to focus on specific genres of painting, which included history paintings based on religious or secular literature, portraits, animal paintings, landscapes, cityscapes, still lives, and depictions of everyday occurrences which came to be known as genre scenes in the eighteenth century.[98] Almost all painting types could be broken down into further themes. For example, genre scenes were subdivided into scenes of conversing, dancing, gambling, celebrating, and eating; landscapes into pastoral views, seascapes, and Italianate scenery; and portraits into

[92] Ibid.

[93] Mariet Westermann, *A Worldly Art: The Dutch Republic, 1585-1718* (New York: Harry N. Abrams, Incorporated, 1996), 43.

[94] Ibid, 34.

[95] M.E.W. Boers, "Pieter De Molijn (1597-1661): A Dutch Painter and the Art Market in the Seventeenth Century," *Journal of Historians of Netherlandish Art* (2017): 10.

[96] Maarten Roy Prak, *The Dutch Republic in the Seventeenth Century: The Golden Age* (Cambridge, UK: Cambridge University Press, 2005), 238.

[97] Ibid.

[98] Wayne E. Franits, *Dutch Seventeenth-Century Genre Painting: Its Stylistic and Thematic Evolution* (New Haven and London: Yale University Press, 2004), 3. For further study, see Robert J. Belton, *The Elements of Art* (Kelowna, Canada: The University of British Columbia, 1996).

single portraits, group portraits, and self-portraits.[99] Though not always reflective of artists' interests, perceptions, or artmaking practices, the guidelines of each genre and theme were tacitly obeyed by painters and collectors and espoused by art academies.[100]

Wealthy collectors such as Becker who dictated the exact sizes, prices, and subject matters of their works and who had the luxury of ordering them directly from painters did so through acts of patronage.[101] More commonly, though, Dutch middle-class customers, particularly in Holland, visited painters' studios to select finished or unfinished works to purchase, as this was a less costly alternative to orchestrating the compositions of the works from the outset.[102] When not bringing customers into their workshops and selling internally, painters, namely Leyster and those in the orbit of Hals, sold their works through art dealers, book shops, picture stores, lotteries, local auctions, personal connections, and annual town fairs in Holland, which permitted painters to sell outside of their guilds in any town of their choosing.[103]

As has been delineated, hierarchies dictated the statuses of both artists and collectors. More precisely, day laborers and peasants encompassed the lower social tiers while burghers and wealthy citizens comprised the upper ones. A comparable hierarchy designed by Samuel van Hoogstraten, a pupil of Rembrandt, emulated the ranking of literary genres (tragic literature was placed first, followed by pastoral romance, comedies, and farce) in order to categorize the abovementioned painting types (history paintings, portraits, genre scenes, landscapes, and still lives) according to their display value and ability to convey morals.[104] This ranking dominated

---

[99] Linda Stone-Ferrier, "An Assessment of Recent Scholarship on Seventeenth-Century Dutch Genre Imagery" in Wayne E. Franits' *The Ashgate Research Companion to Dutch Art of the Seventeenth Century* (New York: Routledge, 2016), 73.
[100] Norbert Schneider, *Still Life* (Cologne: Taschen, 2003), 9.
[101] Mariet Westermann, *A Worldly Art: The Dutch Republic, 1585-1718* (New York: Harry N. Abrams, Incorporated, 1996), 40.
[102] Ibid, 39.
[103] Frima Fox Hofrichter, *Judith Leyster, 1609–1660* (Washington, DC: National Gallery of Art, 2009), 7.
[104] Gillian Perry and Colin Cunningham, *Academies, Museums, and Canons of Art* (New Haven: Yale University Press, 1999), 22. For further study, see Thijs Weststeijn, *The Universal Art of Samuel van Hoogstraten (1627-1678): Painter, Writer, and Courtier* (Amsterdam: Amsterdam University Press,

art academy doctrines into the late nineteenth century.[105] More importantly, for the purposes of this thesis, the ranking of painting genres will show how Leyster's works, by not fitting neatly into either the portrait or genre scene category, defied the bounds of the hierarchy. This will subsequently set the stage for demarcating expressive components of seventeenth-century portraits and genre scenes and which of those features Leyster chose to amalgamate in her paintings.

DUTCH INDIVIDUALISM, PORTRAITURE, AND THE HIERARCHY OF GENRES

To convey morals in a clear, concise manner, the representation of figures was considered a vital element and the highest form of art. History paintings, with their inclusions of figures and portrayals of important religious and historical narratives, were considered most efficient at relaying morals, as well as moving viewers and depicting gesture and expression (particularly if several figures were present).[106] Second most efficient were portraits. They did not portray storylines or challenge painters to exercise their imaginations in the way that history paintings did, but still included figures that could serve functions and immortalized them in the same manner that history paintings preserved events.[107] The rendering of these figures, however, according to Renaissance theoreticians, only necessitated technical proficiency in replicating, copying, and transcribing the surface of the world (unlike history paintings, which

2013); Thijs Weststeijn, *The Visible World: Samuel van Hoogstraten's Art Theory and the Legitimation of Painting in the Dutch Golden Age* (Amsterdam: Amsterdam University Press, 2008); Celeste Brusati, *Artifice and Illusion: The Art and Writing of Samuel van Hoogstraten* (Chicago: University of Chicago Press, 1995).
[105] Ibid.
[106] Gillian Perry and Colin Cunningham, *Academies, Museums, and Canons of Art* (New Haven: Yale University Press, 1999), 22.
[107] Mariet Westermann, *A Worldly Art: The Dutch Republic, 1585-1718* (New York: Harry N. Abrams, Incorporated, 1996), 64, 164.

captured the essence or spirit of the world), hence another reason that portraits were considered second-tier works.[108] After portraiture was the genre picture. Although genre scenes contained figures and narrative elements as well as symbols and metaphors embodying proverbs, the images of everyday life sometimes contained debauchery, rowdiness, and disorderliness; they were therefore considered inferior to images of significant religious or historical events and dignified, distinguished portraits. Works generally absent of figures altogether, such as landscapes and still lives (which were considered overly-concerned with plain material items), were deemed least capable of conveying morals and therefore ranked the lowest in the painting genre hierarchy.[109]

This ranking of painting genres according to their abilities (or lack-thereof) to portray morals was manifested in the order and ways in which works were exhibited, otherwise known as display value. As the most esteemed painting genre, and due to the large-size canvases, history paintings were given prominent, eye-level display at academies, salons, and shops. Portraits were generally hung above history paintings, followed by genre scenes and landscapes at the highest levels, which were furthest from collectors' eyes. Due to their small, portable sizes, still lives were primarily executed for domestic ownership. Artists' reputations coincided with the types of painting they indulged in, and reputations had immediate effects on the prices works fetched at market and on the works' values.[110] Paintings that could be made in less than a day and using low production costs were seen as requiring little effort, whereas the opposite was true of works that necessitated more time and higher production costs.[111] The more difficult a painting was to produce, the higher the artist's reputation was, and the more he or she could

---

[108] Joanna Woods-Marsden, *Renaissance Self-Portraiture* (New Haven and London: Yale University Press, 1998), 193.; Laura R. Bass, *The Drama of the Portrait: Theater and Visual Culture in Early Modern Spain* (University Park: Penn State University Press, 2009), 36.
[109] Norbert Schneider, *Still Life* (Cologne: Taschen, 2003), 7-8.
[110] M.E.W. Boers, "Pieter De Molijn (1597-1661): A Dutch Painter and the Art Market in the Seventeenth Century," *Journal of Historians of Netherlandish Art* (2017): 9.
[111] Ibid.

demand at market.[112] With the hierarchy of genres in mind, the implications of Leyster's consolidations of portraits and everyday scenes grow more intriguing. By combining genres with opposing reputations, Leyster rendered ambiguous the status of her images, tested the limits of the hierarchy, and possibly cultivated fluidity between the different social tastes within the art market, as portraits and genre scenes appealed to individuals from across social strata.

Identifying exactly which elements of each painting type Leyster combined necessitates overviews of the conventions and use of expression in seventeenth-century portraits and genre scenes. Already in the fifteenth century, self-portraits by non-elite artists ushered in a movement away from noble portrayals and towards pictorial autobiographies and explorations of expression.[113] A proliferation of diaries, memoirs, and self-reflective writings accompanied the growth of portraiture and self-portraiture, as both platforms of expression promoted the belief that the individual, rather than being one of a myriad of human souls beneath God, was a being worthy of study, documentation, and interest for his or her own sake.[114] This newfound self-assurance stemmed from several intricate social, religious, and philosophical occurrences in the Netherlands during the seventeenth century, such as the Protestant Reformation, the construction of the Dutch Republic following the Eighty Years' War, and the cultivation of empirical science and philosophy.[115]

After the Eighty Years' War (1568-1648), seven rebellious Dutch provinces gained independence, formed a republic that encompasses most of the present-day Netherlands (Holland), and appointed a *stadhouder* ("keeper of cities") as leader, who was usually a prince descended from William I of Orange, the frontrunner of the revolt.[116] The Southern Netherlands (modern-day Belgium) remained under the control of the Spanish government and Catholic

---

[112] Ibid.
[113] Mariet Westermann, *Rembrandt* (London: Phaidon Press, 2000), 9.
[114] Ibid, 10-11.
[115] Ibid, 11.
[116] Jonathan Israel, *The Dutch Republic: Its Rise, Greatness, and Fall, 1477–1806* (Oxford: Clarendon Press, 1995), 404-406, 596-597.

Church.[117] Though the Dutch Republic did not adhere to a state religion, most of the country practiced Calvinism, as the leaders who had advocated for the independence of the provinces were Calvinists.[118] Characteristics of seventeenth-century Dutch Calvinism include the identification of nature as a predecessor to the hereafter, notions of combining the perceived natural and mystical spheres, extreme distrust of worldly goods and pleasures, and preoccupations with creation, Incarnation, salvation by grace, participation in the Eucharist, and the human race as the corporeal manifestation of divine action.[119] Therefore, due to these Calvinist principles, pride in the country's autonomy, importance given to human culture in relation to the divine, and a focus on individual accountability were fostered throughout the nation.[120]

Protestantism had a direct effect on the Dutch art market as well. Between 100,000 to 150,000 skilled workers and professionals fled religious persecution in the Spanish Netherlands after 1585 and settled in the northern Netherlands, where they comprised approximately ten percent of the region's population by the 1590s.[121] As a result of this migration, Haarlem alone more than doubled in population from 14,000 to 39,000 people by 1622.[122] Since many of those who emigrated brought with them financial and business experience, new industries, saleable operations, and trading networks were established.[123] For a small-sized locale, Haarlem blossomed with a large population and a healthy economy.[124] This was the city into which Leyster was born in 1609 as well as the society for which she would paint her best works.

---

[117] Ibid.
[118] Ibid.
[119] Tony Maan, "Material Culture and Popular Calvinist Worldliness in the Dutch 'Golden Age,'" *History Compass* 9 (2011): 287-88, 293; Hubert Dreyfus and Mark A. Wrathall, *A Companion to Phenomenology and Existentialism* (Hoboken, NJ: Wiley, 2009), 561.
[120] Jonathan Israel, *The Dutch Republic: Its Rise, Greatness, and Fall, 1477–1806* (Oxford: Clarendon Press, 1995), 13.
[121] Deborah Hutton and Rebecca Tucker, "The Worldly Artist in the Seventeenth Century: The Travels of Cornelis Claesz. Heda," *Art History* 37.5 (2014): 865.
[122] Ibid.
[123] Ibid.
[124] Ibid.

In conjunction with Protestantism and the formation of the Dutch Republic, Dutch scientists strove to identify the relationship between humans, the world, and God through empirical research and observation "from life."[125] Invariably, the research led scientists to conclude that humans had an advantaged position amongst God's creations.[126] These findings complemented the rationalist philosophy of René Descartes, whose "I think, therefore I am" assertion, published in nearby Leiden in 1637, encapsulates the nature of the human self and conscience.[127] This, incidentally, was the same decade in which Leyster would paint her *Self Portrait*, which will be the focus of the next two chapters.

Since science and empirical philosophy were considered inseparable, and each field led to analogous conclusions regarding humans as privileged beings, the same interest in individuals and their thoughts that punctuated the religious and political spheres flourished within these realms of study as well. As a result, expression in portraiture and self-portraiture reflected this newfound, widespread interest. Artists began honing elegance, bright colors, and expensive fashions once reserved for nobles, as well as painterly brushstrokes, explorations of light and shadow, direct gazes toward the viewer, and poses and backgrounds tailored to the sitter's private and public personhoods.[128] Leyster's portraits are no exception: her explorations of expression emerged from the independent spirit of the Protestant milieu. Like the many diaries, memoirs, and self-reflective writings that arose during this period, Leyster's self-portrait is similarly autobiographical in that it portrays the painter as the main character in a narrative about an artist's extraordinary ability to bestow life and expression upon ordinary elements. At the same time, Leyster's works, which are notable for their bright colors, costumes, direct gazes,

[125] Simon Schama, "Wives and Wantons: Versions of Womanhood in 17th Century Dutch Art," *The Oxford Art Journal* 3 (1980): 7.
[126] Mariet Westermann, *Rembrandt* (London: Phaidon Press, 2000), 13.
[127] René Descartes, *Discourse on the Method of Rightly Conducting One's Reason and of Seeking Truth in the Sciences* (Leiden: René Descartes, 1637).
[128] Mariet Westermann, *A Worldly Art: The Dutch Republic, 1585-1718* (New York: Harry N. Abrams, Incorporated, 1996), 131, 138, 151.

and specific poses, manage to stray from convention via her versatility, confident flaunting of skill, and meshing of portraits and genre scenes.

THE WORK OF WOMEN

Genre painting could be subdivided into scenes of conversing, dancing, gambling, celebrating, and eating. Another facet of such works was their influence on and critique of the domestic realm governed by women, mothers, maids, and wives, which could be portrayed positively, negatively, or ambiguously.[129] Whereas seventeenth-century portraiture was rooted in Protestant values, domestic genre scenes had their basis in sermons and handbooks on domestic behavior, which was primarily directed toward women (although archetypes of femininity had effects on men and apposite masculinity as well).[130] Writer Jacob Cats held the prevailing Calvinist-inspired opinions that husbands and wives were equal, companionship was a chief reason for marriage, and procreation was merely a consequence of said companionships.[131] These beliefs are conspicuous in two poems by Cats. Aptly paired with a print by Adriaen van de Veene (1589-1662) that depicts a bride receiving guests (fig. 9), Cat's marital poem reads as follows: "Hear, daughter, no ring, party, crown, or herb, but true love makes the bride."[132]

---

[129] Linda Stone-Ferrier, "An Assessment of Recent Scholarship on Seventeenth-Century Dutch Genre Imagery" in Wayne E. Franits' *The Ashgate Research Companion to Dutch Art of the Seventeenth Century* (New York: Routledge, 2016), 81.
[130] Ibid.
[131] Martine van Elk, *Early Modern Women's Writing: Domesticity, Privacy, and the Public Sphere in England and the Dutch Republic* (New York: Springer International Publishing, 2017), 41. For further study, see Gerard Koot, *The Portrayal of Women in Dutch Art of the Dutch Golden Age: Courtship, Marriage and Old Age* (Amherst: University of Massachusetts Press, 2015); Hendrik J. Horn, *The Golden Age Revisited: Arnold Houbraken and a Tale of Two Books* (Doornspijk, Netherlands: Davaco Publishers, 2000); Laurinda S. Dixon, *Women and Illness in Pre-Enlightenment Art and Medicine* (Ithaca, NY: Cornell University Press, 2019).
[132] Jacob Cats quoted in Janny Venema's *Kiliaen van Rensselaer (1586-1643): Designing a New World* (Albany, NY: SUNY Press, 2011), 119.

Similarly, the following poem by Cats exudes a lenient, even divinely endorsed, view of newlyweds:

> It would appear that even God finds some delight
> When from a pure desire married folk will frolic,
> What is not fit in others, and cannot be approved,
> Is accepted of the married couple, without blame.[133]

Other writers, however, maintained the conviction that women were the weaker sex and emphasized the separate spheres and strengths of each gender, as exemplified by a poem published in 1659 by Johan van Nyenborch:

> And each carries out its work and watches over its affairs,
> The women in the house, and the men on the street:
> The woman goes to market, so her family and servants
> Are kept from any want...[134]

Convention dictated that women's primary duties were to rear children, adhere to decorum, manage household monies while husbands tended to commercial matters, and keep clean and well-furnished homes.[135] According to Simon Schama, in the Dutch Republic, the home stood for a respite from the lack of Christian virtue and depravity of the external world, a microcosm of the relative stability and affluence of the government, wealth and social standing (especially when decorated entrance halls were visible to public onlookers), and a place of congregation for neighbors, friends, and family, further solidifying its impact on the social lives of seventeenth-century Dutch burghers.[136] To illustrate his thesis, Schama references a seventeenth-century engraving by the female artist Geertruyd Rogman (1625-1657) titled *Woman Sewing* from 1640-

---

[133] Jacob Cats quoted in Ton Hoenselaars' and Rui Carvalho Homem's *Translating Shakespeare for the Twenty-First Century* (Amsterdam, Netherlands: Rodopi, 2004), 84.

[134] Johan van Nyenborch quoted in Elizabeth Alice Honig's "Desire and Domestic Economy," *The Art Bulletin* 83 (2001): 306. For further study, see Gerard Koot, *The Portrayal of Women in Dutch Art of the Dutch Golden Age: Courtship, Marriage and Old Age* (Amherst: University of Massachusetts Press, 2015).

[135] Julia Skelly, *The Uses of Excess in Visual and Material Culture, 1600-2010* (Philadelphia: Taylor & Francis, 2014), 72-3.

[136] Simon Schama, "Wives and Wantons: Versions of Womanhood in 17th Century Dutch Art," *The Oxford Art Journal* 3 (1980): 8-9.

57 (fig. 10).[137] In the image, one woman is shown intently sewing while the other pauses what she is doing to glance at her companion. Commonplace vanitas emblems, such as candles, clocks, skulls, and spindles, are present. Rather than being the central focus of the work, though, the objects appear as though they were placed in the room by happenchance.[138] The vanitas theme is subordinate to the representation of the productivity of the women—both the subjects within the image and the female artist herself. As a result, the image manages to demonstrate the decency and stability of the Dutch household while simultaneously fostering the independent sensibility that was generated by female artists from the period.[139]

The imagery produced by female artists, while similar in theme to works by their male counterparts, were nevertheless often different in tone and in their attention to the value of women's work; for male artists, however, representations of women were often an occasion to moralize, such as by upholding monogamy. Since men possessed social and economic benefits necessary for expedient marriages and subsequently the foundations of households, monogamy was of utmost importance.[140] Violations of the sanctity of marriage via cuckoldry, illegitimate births, and other forms of debauchery were often humorously depicted in genre scenes in which midwives and nurses gossiped about such matters.[141] Utter chaos and disorderliness made for comedic domestic genre scenes that humorously accepted the human condition while reinforcing the opposite, proper scenarios as idyllic depictions of love, family, and home.[142]

For example, in Jan Steen's *In Luxury, Look Out* from 1663 (fig. 11), the antithesis of the happy family is humorously portrayed. The lady of the house has fallen asleep at the table on the left, thus allowing complete chaos to ensue. A "loose" woman in the foreground holds a filled

---

[137] Ibid, 5.
[138] Ibid.
[139] Ibid.
[140] Mariet Westermann, *A Worldly Art: The Dutch Republic, 1585-1718* (New York: Harry N. Abrams, Incorporated, 1996), 120.
[141] Ibid.
[142] Linda Stone-Ferrier, "An Assessment of Recent Scholarship on Seventeenth-Century Dutch Genre Imagery" in Wayne E. Franits' *The Ashgate Research Companion to Dutch Art of the Seventeenth Century* (New York: Routledge, 2016), 84.

glass between the legs of the man of the house while he grins at a nun, a dog eats a meat pie that fell from the table, a child pilfers an object from the cabinet on the wall, a boy tries out a pipe, a child in a highchair plays with a string of pearls, and a young man tries to play the violin, among other scenarios and references to Dutch proverbs. In short, comedic images offered both negative portrayals of the lowlier aspects of middle-class life that viewers could laugh at, but should ultimately avoid, as well as positive portrayals with which middle-class viewers could more easily identify.[143]

Unlike the large cast of characters, boisterous motifs, disruptive angles and diagonals, jarring color juxtapositions, and loose brushwork used in comedic genre scenes, there were also more serious images featuring quiet interiors with clear light, harmonious primary colors, straightforward lines and angles, and singular figures engaged in housework.[144] By having stable compositions, serious domestic scenes invited contemplation of the integrity and righteousness of seventeenth-century Dutch life.[145] Adriaen van Ostade's *Prayer Before the Meal* from 1653 (fig. 12) serves as a fine example. A mother and father are shown praying before their children, thereby setting a virtuous example for them and exhibiting gratitude for simplistic joys. In the moralizing domestic genre, the role of virtuous Dutch women was to stabilize the household.[146] Taught to spin, sew, and make lace, women in the Republic not only honed these skills for their households, but also supplemented their families' incomes by selling yarn, cloth and lace, and even sometimes (albeit rarely) forming their own guilds of textile workers within the male guild system.[147]

The women in these moralizing scenes by male artists, however, do not paint; significantly, Leyster does not portray herself undertaking any of these activities. This gendering of the home was reflected in pictures and prescribed by the masculine definition of most civic

---

[143] Mariet Westermann, *A Worldly Art: The Dutch Republic, 1585-1718* (New York: Harry N. Abrams, Incorporated, 1996), 122.
[144] Ibid, 122, 124.
[145] Ibid, 124.
[146] Ibid.
[147] Ibid, 125.

space.[148] Apart from occasional depictions of women perusing markets, purchasing food, and strolling through streets as part of an extension of the home, "good" Dutch women were only shown performing housework while men were pictorially depicted engaged in matters pertaining to financial, governmental, and social exchange.[149] Even when depicted indoors, men were shown preoccupied with erudition, diplomacy, accounting, sermons, and other activities that sustained connections with the exterior sphere.[150] These gendered roles applied to other painted settings as well, such as taverns, gambling establishments, and brothels where not-so-good Dutch women appear.[151]

While men indulged in hobbies and pastimes, women, even when portrayed as immodest or uncouth participants, regulated these settings to a degree.[152] For instance, in Gerrit ter Borch's *Woman Drinking Wine with a Drunken Soldier* from 1658-1659 (fig. 13), an inebriated soldier succumbs to his drunken state as the woman sitting beside him continues to drink. Moreover, despite being an active participant in the debauchery, the woman remains cognizant and alert while the man relinquishes all control of his sensibilities. By regulating these settings (both literally and in images), one might argue that women in the seventeenth-century Dutch Republic enjoyed a certain degree of independence.[153] This claim will be examined below.

Despite the black-and-white depiction of good, virtuous Dutch women at home and scandalous Dutch women in taverns, actual Dutch women of the seventeenth century enjoyed

---

[148] Jennifer Spinks and Susan Broomhall, *Early Modern Women in the Low Countries: Feminizing Sources and Interpretations of the Past* (Farnham, UK: Ashgate Publishing, 2011), 45. For further study, see Marjorie E. Wieseman, Wayne E. Franits, and H. Perry Chapman, *Vermeer's Women: Secrets and Silence* (New Haven: Yale University Press, 2011).
[149] Elizabeth Alice Honig, "Desire and Domestic Economy," *The Art Bulletin* 83 (2001): 309.; Linda Stone-Ferrier, "An Assessment of Recent Scholarship on Seventeenth-Century Dutch Genre Imagery" in Wayne E. Franits' *The Ashgate Research Companion to Dutch Art of the Seventeenth Century* (New York: Routledge, 2016), 81. For further study, see Gerard Koot, *The Portrayal of Women in Dutch Art of the Dutch Golden Age: Courtship, Marriage and Old Age* (Amherst: University of Massachusetts Press, 2015) ; Marjorie E. Wieseman, Wayne E. Franits, and H. Perry Chapman, *Vermeer's Women: Secrets and Silence* (New Haven: Yale University Press, 2011).
[150] Mariet Westermann, *A Worldly Art: The Dutch Republic, 1585-1718* (New York: Harry N. Abrams, Incorporated, 1996), 125.
[151] Ibid.
[152] Ibid, 126.
[153] Martha Moffitt Peacock, "Geertruydt Roghman and the Female Perspective in 17th-Century Dutch Genre Imagery," *Woman's Art Journal* 14 (1993-1994): 8.

greater independence than their counterparts in England, for instance. Compared to England, many more Dutch households were governed by single females. According to contemporary letters and journals of visitors to the Netherlands, Dutch women were not only permitted to decline the sexual advances of their husbands if there were evidence or reason to believe that a physical encounter would lead to the transmission of syphilis or other venereal diseases, they could also take communion alongside men and receive and possess property even while their spouses were still alive.[154] Letters that expressed consternation at these liberties reflect the fact that many Dutch men likely felt threatened by the liberties their women held and by the possibility of their usurpation of customary male roles.[155]

Leyster utilized the gaiety and loose brushwork of comedic genre scenes that feature controversial Dutch women as well as the clear light and harmonious primary colors of serious ones that contain upright Dutch women, but deviated from these conventions in two important ways. As a member of the guild and as a female painter contending with such great male contemporaries as Rembrandt, Johannes Vermeer, and Hals, Leyster was undoubtedly progressive as an artist. Yet in spite of this status, she de-emphasized gender-specific perspectives and instead showcased her ability to take on a range of subjects and her capacity to work in a variety of popular styles so as to meet the demands of the market and compete with her male colleagues.[156] Another innovation in her genre scenes was her minimization of narrative elements in favor of emphasizing poses, momentary gestures, and expressions. Considering that her works are the result of meshing portraitures with genre scenes, her amalgamations of the two painting categories are so seamless that they obscure the exact definitions of each one, overlapping their qualities and generating a type all her own. This type, as we shall see in the following chapter, cultivated expression in a way that upended the male-

---

[154] Ibid; Simon Schama, "Wives and Wantons: Versions of Womanhood in 17th Century Dutch Art," *The Oxford Art Journal* 3 (1980): 6.
[155] Martha Moffitt Peacock, "Geertruydt Roghman and the Female Perspective in 17th-Century Dutch Genre Imagery," *Woman's Art Journal* 14 (1993 -1994): 8.
[156] James A. Welu and Pieter Biesboer, *Judith Leyster: A Dutch Master and Her World* (Worcester: Waanders Printers, Zwolle, 1993), 12.

centric settings of traditional Dutch art. Images were meant to inculcate women and keep them in their place. However, they may have sometimes had the reverse effect, especially when the artist was a woman herself. The result potentially increased women's conspicuousness and significance and accentuated the need for adept, autonomous, and knowledgeable women in seventeenth-century Dutch Protestant, middle-class society.[157] While Leyster did not focus on her gender by centering only on the depiction of women, she nonetheless displayed a self-possession that channeled the abovementioned Dutch female autonomy.

EXPRESSION IN THE ARTS

Earlier, Leyster's distinctive expressions were said to have been later codified in an academic context by Charles Le Brun's lecture, *The Expression of the Passions* (1688), published almost three decades after Leyster's lifetime. The significance of elucidating this codification shall be to reveal its indirect testament to the spontaneity and candidness produced by Leyster's experimental use of expression in the overlapping of painting categories. While Le Brun did not refer specifically to Leyster's paintings, he was deeply interested in emotion in art, hence his codification of their visual manifestations.[158] The most influential artist in France from the mid- to late-seventeenth century, Le Brun reached the pinnacle of his career by 1660, the year of Leyster's death.[159] Having been given the positions of First Painter to the King in 1661 and director of the Académie Royale in 1663, Le Brun exercised administrative control of the training of all artists in Paris as well as the dissemination of the most noteworthy commissions

---

[157] Martha Moffitt Peacock, "Geertruydt Roghman and the Female Perspective in 17th-Century Dutch Genre Imagery," *Woman's Art Journal* 14 (1993 -1994): 8.
[158] Ann Sutherland Harris, *Seventeenth-Century Art & Architecture* (Upper Saddle River, NJ: Pearson Education, Inc., 2005), 303.
[159] Ibid 304.

conferred by Louis XIV and his court.[160] By coordinating the Sun King's public persona at Versailles, Le Brun's career was officially launched.[161] Of the several phases of Le Brun's career as a painter, his large altarpieces and battle pieces from the second half of the 1660s for King Louis XIV were his most famous works.[162] During his career, he also helped to situate visual arts at the center of French politics and established the French Royal Academy of Painting and Sculpture, which produced hundreds of well-trained painters, sculptors, and craftsmen for the next century as well as the hierarchy of genres described in the previous chapter.[163]

Though an excellent portraitist and draughtsman, Le Brun viewed any genre other than history painting to be a mere tool for refining technical prowess, as only history paintings could transform the moral significances of events into comprehensible images of human valor and virtue.[164] To digest history paintings, spectators were responsible for taking the time to "read" each figure's face and gesture, hence why Le Brun was intensely invested in expression in his lecture at the Academy, which he delivered between 1668 and 1670.[165] Le Brun's belief that history paintings need be comprehendible stemmed from a desire to reconcile conflicting ideas about what was required of an artist to properly construct emotions through images on canvases.[166] Seventeenth-century painters were frequently required to represent subjects such as agonizing deaths during historical battles as well as saints in ecstasy and in the triumph of martyrdom, all of which were emotional events that were unlikely to have been witnessed by the artists in person.[167]

---

[160] Ibid.
[161] Ibid, 307.
[162] Ibid, 304.
[163] Ibid, 309.
[164] Ibid, 306.
[165] Ibid 306; on this, see also Jennifer Montagu, *The Expression of the Passions: The Origin and Influence of Charles Le Brun's Conference sur l'expression generale et particuliere* (New Haven and London: Yale University Press, 1994), 141.
[166] Jennifer Montagu, *The Expression of the Passions: The Origin and Influence of Charles Le Brun's Conference sur l'expression generale et particuliere* (New Haven and London: Yale University Press, 1994), 6.
[167] Ibid.

Representing passions such as joy, wonder, anger, or surprise required understanding of the most rudimentary mental and physical principles behind each one, which Le Brun believed could be visibly manifested via facial movements and expressions.[168] Upon understanding how to accurately represent each passion, Le Brun believed that he would be able to efficaciously strike a balance between grasping the workings of nature and devising entirely new worlds on canvases.[169] He sought to improve upon nature, causing the passions of the soul to be free of obscurities and hindrances, and, above all, be easily identifiable.[170]

> Expression, in my opinion, is a simple and natural image of the thing we wish to represent; it is a necessary ingredient of all the parts of painting, and without it no picture can be perfect; it is this which indicates the true character of each object; it is by this means that the different natures of bodies are distinguished, that figures seem to have movement, and everything which is imitated appears to be real.[171]

These principles held by Le Brun were intimately linked to seventeenth-century philosopher, mathematician, and scientist René Descartes, who described the passions at great length in *The Passions of the Soul* (1637).[172] Le Brun took Descartes's descriptions and demonstrated how emotions manifested themselves externally, instituting a direct connection between the passions and the movement of facial muscles and articulating the laws of facial expression.[173] These

---

[168] Alain Mérot, *French Painting in the Seventeenth Century* (New Haven: Yale University Press, 1995), 267.

[169] Jennifer Montagu, *The Expression of the Passions: The Origin and Influence of Charles Le Brun's Conference sur l'expression generale et particuliere* (New Haven and London: Yale University Press, 1994), 7, 30, 8.

[170] Ibid, 7.

[171] Le Brun quoted in Ibid, 26.

[172] Benjamin Tilghman, *Reflections on Aesthetic Judgment and Other Essays* (Farnham, UK: Ashgate Publishing, 2006), 87. For further study, see Charles Le Brun, *A Method to Learn to Design the Passions* (Los Angeles: William Andrews Clark Memorial Library, 1980); Rene Descartes, *The Passions of the Soul* (Paris: Rene Descartes, 1637).

[173] Jennifer Montagu, *The Expression of the Passions: The Origin and Influence of Charles Le Brun's Conference sur l'expression generale et particuliere* (New Haven and London: Yale University Press, 1994), 7.

Cartesian laws were then outlined as a template for subsequent Academy artists to follow in his lecture, *The Expression of the Passions*.[174]

If Descartes was a direct influence on Le Brun, Leyster might be considered here as an indirect one. Many of Leyster's works contain figures of children and animals (to be discussed in Chapters 3 and 4) while few, if any, of Le Brun's codified expressions were those of children or animals. For these reasons, Leyster's paintings remain highly valuable and distinctive points of study. Before expressions became codified and regarded as mere tools to demonstrate technical prowess, Leyster crafted spontaneous, sincere expressions, including in the innocent figures of children and animals, which broadened the possibilities of portraits and genre scenes. The next chapter will look at the nuanced exploration of human expression in Leyster's *Self Portrait*, painted some two years before Descartes' treatise on the soul.

---

[174] When the lecture was delivered to the Academy by Le Brun, it was met with praise, published in sixty-three separate editions, and remained the tenet on expression in Europe for two centuries. Modern scholars at the turn of the last century, however, attacked Le Brun for discouraging artists to draw what they saw before them, writing like a physiologist rather than an aesthetician, being divorced from nature, and misunderstanding the principles of the passions upon which his beliefs rested. Although most of these critiques have since been disregarded by contemporary scholars, one remains persistent, and that is the dislike of the stiffness of the figures in some of his paintings. Due to his codification of expressions, Le Brun's figures are sometimes thought to lack spontaneity and genuine human emotion, which modern viewers seek in the works of Le Brun's predecessors, contemporaries, and successors. On this, see: Mosche Barasch, *Modern Theories of Art 2: From Impressionism to Kandinsky* (New York: NYU Press, 1998), 94-95; Jennifer Montagu, *The Expression of the Passions: The Origin and Influence of Charles Le Brun's Conférence sur l'expression generale et particuliere* (New Haven and London: Yale University Press, 1994), 6; Ann Sutherland Harris, *Seventeenth-Century Art & Architecture* (Upper Saddle River, NJ: Pearson Education, Inc., 2005), 307.

Chapter 2: Judith Leyster's *Self Portrait* in Comparison to Other Self-Portraits by Contemporary Male Artists and Female Predecessors

Of the works that encompass Leyster's oeuvre, her *Self Portrait* from 1635 is perhaps her best-known painting and one of the greatest windows into her adroitness at honing expression and challenging the boundaries of portraiture. This work will be explored in comparison to similar self-portraits by contemporary male artists and female antecedents so as to emphasize its innovative characteristics. In all portraiture, tacit dialogues exist between the painters and the sitters, the two most vital constituents.[175] Whereas some dialogues uncover social disparities between artists and their wealthy subjects, self-portraiture differs in that the artist and model are one and the same. The conversation occurs between self and self, and both the subject's appearance and painter's rendering of it are the synonymous focus.[176] How this appearance is related to that of the artist's self-image and mirror image (in other words, the intersection of the "I," the "me," and the artwork) is the foundation of all self-portraiture.[177]

LEYSTER'S MALE PEERS

Many self-portraits by Leyster's male contemporaries depict the artists seated at easels, such as *Self-Portrait of an Artist Seated at an Easel* attributed to Cornelis Bisschop from circa 1653 (fig. 14), *Self-Portrait (?) at an Easel* ascribed to Gerrit Dou from circa 1628–29 (fig. 15),

---

[175] Joanna Woods-Marsden, *Renaissance Self-Portraiture* (New Haven and London: Yale University Press, 1998), 25.
[176] Ibid, 27.
[177] Ibid.

and *Artist at His Easel* attributed to Gerrit Dou from circa 1630–32 (fig. 16). In all three works, the artists turn toward the viewer while seated before canvases, their sharp gazes implying a sense of immediacy and informality. Their canvases face away from the viewer, leaving one to question whether self-portraits or, in the case of the oversized canvas in Dou's *Self-Portrait (?) at an Easel*, a history painting is being rendered. Dou's works are also filled with worldly, cultured, and some vanitas objects that tie the artist to erudite external affairs. These objects, coupled with the large-scale painting within the painting in Dou's *Self-Portrait (?) at an Easel*, raise and reinforce the male artist's authority across all genres.

Rembrandt's *Artist in his Studio* from 1628 (fig. 17), arguably one of the most well-known portraits of an artist situated before his easel, not only underlines male authority through the inclusion of a large-scale canvas presumed to be a history painting, but also refers to the splendor of the act of painting as a whole. Many believe the artist to be Rembrandt himself, which is not implausible, although some scholars think this to be unlikely.[178] What remains clear, though, is that Rembrandt identified with the painter depicted in the scene.[179] This figure of a painter wears a slightly-out-of-date *tabard* (housecoat) and holds a brush while stepping back to contemplate his work, which is supported by an easel in the foreground that faces away from viewers at an askew angle.[180] Both the painting and the painter are positioned as if from the viewpoint of the sitter.[181] Whereas the back of the canvas is cloaked in shadow, the painter is basked in light, all of which is composed of impasto brushstrokes that lend illusionism to the wooden floor and plaster walls and add texture for its own sake, as Paul Barolsky and Lawrence Geddes have argued.[182] Tension abounds between the engulfing size of the canvas within the

---

[178] Paul Barolsky and Lawrence Goedde, "Ambiguity in Rembrandt's Boston Artist in His Studio," *Notes in the History of Art* 30 (Summer 2011): 45.
[179] Ibid, 45.
[180] Ibid, 43, 45.
[181] Joanna Woods-Marsden, *Renaissance Self-Portraiture* (New Haven and London: Yale University Press, 1998), 25.
[182] Paul Barolsky and Lawrence Goedde, "Ambiguity in Rembrandt's Boston Artist in His Studio," *Notes in the History of Art* 30 (Summer 2011): 43.

image and the small size of the image itself, creating a fascinating ambiguity of scale.[183] The figure of the painter, who is situated deep in the background while the canvas and easel occupy the foreground, is dwarfed by his art, thus alluding to the grandeur of his creation and to the act of painting in general.[184] Adding to the grandiose status of painting is the monumental size of the canvas within the image, suggesting to some that it contains a history scene.[185] The exact subject, however, remains unknown. In the male self-portraits in front of easels that have been presented thus far, the canvases are shrouded in literal and metaphorical darkness, leaving viewers infinitely wishing to enter the spaces and contemplate what the painters behold.[186]

Against this tradition, Leyster succeeded in challenging her role as a female artist. By experimenting with expression in portraiture, she displayed skill and inventiveness. Leyster's self-portrait reveals the canvas where she is in the act of painting a man. This places full creative control in her hands and demonstrates her confidence in displaying her craft. Unlike the grave faces of her male counterparts, she smiles open-mouthed and even casually leans back in her chair as she does so. Both her expression and pose would have been considered brazen, as dynamic poses and pronounced facial expressions were rare in portraiture and self-portraiture.[187] Even smiles were uncommon, and those that did appear were close-mouthed and with seldom a flash of teeth.[188] The infrequency of smiles in portraiture may largely be attributed to societal customs and modesty.[189] Due to their rarity, I postulate that some artists may have also experienced difficulties painting them. On a similar note, just as people today encounter trouble holding smiles for photographs for long periods of time, so sitters for portraits may have

---

[183] Ibid.
[184] Paul Barolsky and Lawrence Goedde, "Ambiguity in Rembrandt's Boston Artist in His Studio," *Notes in the History of Art* 30 (Summer 2011): 45; Joanna Woods-Marsden, *Renaissance Self-Portraiture* (New Haven and London: Yale University Press, 1998), 25.
[185] Paul Barolsky and Lawrence Goedde, "Ambiguity in Rembrandt's Boston Artist in His Studio," *Notes in the History of Art* 30 (Summer 2011): 45.
[186] Ibid.
[187] Richard Brilliant, *Portraiture* (London: Reaktion Books, 2004), 10; Sheri Klein, *Art and Laughter* (London: I.B. Tauris, 2006), 33.
[188] Sheri Klein, *Art and Laughter* (London: I.B. Tauris, 2006), 33.
[189] Richard Brilliant, *Portraiture* (London: Reaktion Books, 2004), 10-11; Sheri Klein, *Art and Laughter* (London: I.B. Tauris, 2006), 33.

found it enervating to maintain smiles that appeared relaxed rather than unnatural or obligatory. On close inspection, painted expressions that seem natural and unprompted upon initial glance often appear progressively affected and overformal.[190] Leyster, however, managed to capture both the spontaneity and relaxedness in her bold smile. Frieda van Emden has argued that Leyster seems to have painted herself in one sitting, circumventing all suspicion of tedious posing.[191]

The cheerful musician on her canvas, like a figure from a genre scene, echoes her unabashed smile, ease, and poise. Unlike the hidden canvases in the self-portraits of her male contemporaries, viewers are not left to wonder what is on Leyster's canvas. Nor are we made to guess what kind of picture she is in the act of painting. Instead, observers are boldly confronted with Leyster's skill and mastery of real-life emotion.

We might compare the ingenuity of Leyster's composition with Pieter Claesz's *Vanitas Still Life* from circa 1628 (fig. 18), which is another, more unusual male self-portrait at an easel. The work incorporates the objects seen in Dou's *Artist at His Easel*, but to a more creative extent. The highly-detailed still life, at first glance, portrays a traditional vanitas arrangement, reminding the viewer of imminent death and of the worthlessness of earthly pursuits. The painting consists of, from left to right, a reflective sphere, pocket watch with its back open, extinguished oil lamp, quill, tipped over inkwell, violin with a bow lying across its strings, book, overturned goblet, and skull.[192] Light pouring in from the left-hand side (presumably through a window) illuminates the objects and directs the viewer's focus towards them.

Most apparent of the vanitas objects, however, are the pocket watch, goblet, and skull. According to Mariet Westermann, the watch itself signifies the passage of a lifetime while its

---

[190] Richard Brilliant, *Portraiture* (London: Reaktion Books, 2004), 10.
[191] Frieda van Emden, "Judith Leyster, a Female Frans Hals," *The Art World* 3 (March 1918): 501.
[192] Jelena Todorovic, *The Spaces That Never Were in Early Modern Art: An Exploration of Edges and Frontiers* (Cambridge, UK: Cambridge Scholars Publishing, 2019), 71.

open, viewer-facing back implies that someone attempted to tamper with its mysterious nature.[193] The goblet, without even so much as a single drop of liquid left, testifies to the short-lived quality of earthly pleasures. The skull is what all people will be reduced to after spending their lives pursuing worldly interests, including writing (per the quill and inkwell), literature (reflected by the book), and the arts (embodied by the violin, which also stands for the rivalry between painting and music).

At far left is a glass sphere upon which is reflected some of the objects on the table as well as Claesz in the act of painting the still life. In keeping with the vanitas theme, the sphere's bubble-like form attests to the fragility of human life. However, the presence of Claesz at his easel de-stabilizes the conventional still life painting in that portraits are intended to eternalize their subjects in paint rather than emphasize their passing.[194] By immortalizing himself in the work, the artist also lent alternative meanings to the vanitas symbols. For instance, the watch, whose minute and second hands tick away life's moments, equally encapsulates art's ability to freeze moments in time.[195] Similarly, the quill, inkwell, and book, though transitory earthly pursuits, are tools used to preserve written word. The presence of the self-portrait also elevates the status of still lives and their concern with ordinary things.[196] Claesz wears a sophisticated hat and collar rather than a workshop smock.[197] In so doing, and by donning these clothes in the reflection of an object amongst many, the artist presents painting as a skill equal to those employed in other crafts.[198] In turn, the work is elevated from the lowest tier of the painting

---

[193] Mariet Westermann, *A Worldly Art: The Dutch Republic, 1585-1718* (New York: Harry N. Abrams, Incorporated, 1996), 164.
[194] Pieter Biesboer, Martina Brunner-Bulst, et al., *Pieter Claesz: Master of Haarlem Still Life* (Haarlem: Frans Hals Museum, 2004), 46; Hubert Dreyfus and Mark A. Wrathall, *A Companion to Phenomenology and Existentialism* (Hoboken, NJ: Wiley, 2009), 571.
[195] Pieter Biesboer, Martina Brunner-Bulst, et al., *Pieter Claesz: Master of Haarlem Still Life* (Haarlem: Frans Hals Museum, 2004), 46-7.
[196] Mariet Westermann, *A Worldly Art: The Dutch Republic, 1585-1718* (New York: Harry N. Abrams, Incorporated, 1996), 164.
[197] Ibid.
[198] Ibid.

hierarchy to an example of how complex a still life can be when executed with enormous adroitness and wit.[199]

In much the same manner that Claesz de-stabilized and elevated the still-life genre, Leyster undermined portraiture and elevated genre scenes as well as her own status as an artist. Nonetheless, she did so with the added and greatly-explored element of expression. Her open-mouthed smile, by signifying laughter and movement, conveying self-assurance, proclaiming her place in the male-dominated art world, and paralleling the laughing musician on her canvas, diluted the customary staidness of both portraits and self-portraits. If Claesz's heavy-handed vanitas still life speaks of his serious sense of self, Leyster's white ruffled collar emphasizes her mastery of painting due to its fine detailing and frames her head as if to present her mastery of spontaneous human expression to viewers. Moreover, while she wears a large collar, the ruffles' sheer, wispy, and luminous edges, however, temper the clothing adornment's bulky size. Deep, shining creases in the velvet portions of her dress complement the sheen in her collar, echoing and mimicking a play of light and shadow. Painterly brush strokes visible in the scintillating ruffled collar, coupled with the open mouths, aid in conveying a sense of spontaneity in form and content. This rapid unveiling of personhood, the de-stabilization of the composition, and her openness to the viewer via direct gestures satisfy what Hanneke Grootenboer has defined as theatricality in art.[200] They also demonstrate how she approached her self-image with lightness and joy rather than with a heavy sense of mortality as her male counterparts did.

---

[199] Ibid.
[200] Hanneke Grootenboer, "How to Become a Picture: Theatricality as Strategy in Seventeenth-Century Dutch Portraits," *Art History* 33 (2010): 321-23. For further study, see Michael Fried, *Art and Objecthood: Essays and Reviews* (Chicago: University of Chicago Press, 1998).

Having considered Leyster in relation to her male peers, we now turn to a comparison of Leyster's self-portrait to those of her female predecessors. First, it is integral to note that, during the Renaissance, the thought of women becoming independent professional artists was unfathomable despite the few exceptions.[201] This notion is already expressed in a passage from a treatise on sculpture published in 1504 by Pomponius Gauricus, which reads:

> One [sex] is noble, just, intrepid, audacious, equitable, magnanimous, kind, constant, courageous, honest, liberal, [and] magnificent. The other is base, unjust, fearful, rash, intemperate, indolent, cruel, trying, fickle, always inconstant, dishonest, greedy, [and] good for nothing.[202]

The conviction that women were created inferior to men was so commonplace that Gauricus did not bother to delimit for his readers which sex was gallant and which sordid.[203] This belief was voiced and molded by Western philosophy, art and literature, and those who attempted to break free of it found it challenging to not undermine their self-worth as they had been accustomed to doing, and were relegated to limited audiences, thus making the upcoming female self-portraits all the more exceptional. Unsurprisingly, in accordance with the gender hierarchy, artmaking was considered a male perquisite.[204] Joanna Woods-Marsden has even argued that sketchy brushstrokes, impasto, and scumbling were considered virile maneuvers, while the paintbrush was regarded as a phallic instrument.[205] The paintbrush, or active tool, is dipped into the paint (the passive, feminine element), thereby embodying procreation and solidifying the notion that

---

[201] Joanna Woods-Marsden, *Renaissance Self-Portraiture* (New Haven and London: Yale University Press, 1998), 188.
[202] Gauricus quoted in Ibid, 187.
[203] Ibid.
[204] Fredrika H. Jacobs, "Woman's Capacity to Create: The Unusual Case of Sofonisba Anguissola," *Renaissance Quarterly* 47 (1994): 92.
[205] Joanna Woods-Marsden, *Renaissance Self-Portraiture* (New Haven and London: Yale University Press, 1998), 188.

so man could generate life, so only the male artist could produce great art.[206] Women, even

when actively striving to reverse these roles, were deemed intellectually and biologically

incapable of doing so.[207] The most that they could do was discuss the arts, should the occasion

arise, within domestic spheres (an idea that reflected a minor improvement in attitude toward

women and their artistic endeavors in the mid-sixteenth century).[208]

Those women who managed to work as artists in all-male environs in the fifteenth

through seventeenth centuries were restricted to the portrait and self-portrait genre (Lavinia

Fontana being an extraordinary exception to this rule).[209] Owing to the fact that, over the course

of the Renaissance, women were economically, socially, and intellectually subordinate to fathers

and husbands, the portraits that they did manage to paint reflected their gender restrictions.[210]

Male figures in Northern Renaissance paintings were customarily given more dominating

gestures, glances, and positions.[211] In triptychs and similar formats, men were given the place of

honor and stood to the right of the holy figures (the *dexter* or good side), which was left-of-

center for spectators.[212] By contrast, women traditionally stood to the holy figure's left (*sinister*

or sinful) side, which was right-of-center for viewers, and exhibited body language that was

---

[206] Fredrika H. Jacobs, "Woman's Capacity to Create: The Unusual Case of Sofonisba Anguissola," *Renaissance Quarterly* 47 (1994): 81.
[207] Ibid, 92.
[208] Joanna Woods-Marsden, *Renaissance Self-Portraiture* (New Haven and London: Yale University Press, 1998), 188-190.
[209] Fontana, recognized as Europe's first female painter to attain professional status in direct competition with male artists in her own city, and whose career remarkably continued to burgeon even following her marriage to Gian Paolo Zappi of Imona, painted altarpieces, private devotional works, and mythological scenes as well as portraits of Bolognese scholars and nobles. On this, see: Fredrika H. Jacobs, "Woman's Capacity to Create: The Unusual Case of Sofonisba Anguissola," *Renaissance Quarterly* 47 (1994): 87; Caroline P. Murphy, *Lavinia Fontana: A Painter and her Patrons in Sixteenth-century Bologna* (New Haven and London: Yale University Press, 2003), 1, 38, 162; Vera & Angela Ghirardi Fortunati, *Lavinia Fontana of Bologna, 1552-1614* (Segrate, Italy: Electa, 1998); Leticia Ruiz Gómez, *A Tale of Two Women Painters: Sofonisba Anguissola and Lavinia Fontana* (Madrid: Museo Nacional del Prado, 2019).
[210] Craig Harbison, *The Mirror of the Artist: Northern Renaissance Art in its Historical Context* (Upper Saddle River, NJ: Laurence King Publishing Limited, 1995), 21.
[211] Ibid, 128.
[212] Ibid.

subservient to male figures.[213] Leyster, it should be noted, markedly reversed this compositional convention in her *Self Portrait*.

To circumvent these pictorial limitations, female artists in the sixteenth and seventeenth centuries began developing witty and intelligent portrait techniques. Many of these artists hailed from Italy, a nation strongly tied to the Netherlands via overseas trade relations. Throughout the seventeenth century, almonds, lemons, and rice, for instance, were loaded at Genoa for Dutch ports, while oranges, sulfur, raisins, gall nuts, and cotton were exported and re-exported to Holland from elsewhere in Italy.[214] Patronage between Catholic artists, Protestant patrons, and vice versa also linked the two locations. Nevertheless, as this section illuminates, Leyster's Italian female predecessors further bridged the two regions by devising original portrait compositions that came to be adopted first by Italian artists of the sixteenth century (both male and female alike), and later by Leyster herself.

One such Italian female predecessor of Leyster was Flemish Renaissance painter Caterina van Hemessen. Known primarily for a series of female portraits from the late 1540s and early 1550s as well as a few religious scenes, van Hemessen is often cited as the first painter, regardless of gender, to have created a self-portrait in which the artist is represented sitting at an easel (fig. 19).[215] Admittedly, van Hemessen (like Fontana) was a special case in that she had the advantage of her father being a painter (unlike Leyster, who had no artists in her family), thus she had an easier route into the artistic sphere.[216] Though she was trained by her father, she created a straightforward, realistic style that diverged from his mannered and highly contrived

---

[213] Ibid.

[214] David William Davies, *A Primer of Dutch Seventeenth Century Overseas Trade* (Heidelberg, Germany: Springer Netherlands, 2013), 42.

[215] Susan Frances Jones, *Van Eyck to Gossaert* (London: National Gallery, 2011), 136. For further study, see Jordi Vigue, *Great Women Masters of Art* (New York City: Watson-Guptill, 2003); Frances Borzello, *Seeing Ourselves: Women's Self-Portraits* (New York: Thames & Hudson, 2016).

[216] Craig Harbison, *The Mirror of the Artist: Northern Renaissance Art in its Historical Context* (Upper Saddle River, NJ: Laurence King Publishing Limited, 1995), 21. For further study, see Burr Wallen, *Jan van Hemessen: An Antwerp Painter Between Reform and Counter-Reform* (Ann Arbor, Michigan: UMI Research Press, 1983).

works.[217] In her *Self Portrait* from 1548, the artist cleverly depicted herself about to commence a portrait, her blank canvas (which faces the viewer) on the verge of capturing the artistic inspiration that will pour from her steady hand.[218] She sits against a stark, neutral background, fixing her gaze just beyond the viewer. As with other portraits that are ascribed to her, which are small, quiet, and characterized by realism, this work utilizes a dark background and distant gaze which make for an exalted, intimate portrait.[219] Rather than wear the garb of a painter, van Hemessen adorned herself in sophisticated clothing that elevated her status and connoted modesty. Along with conveying humility, van Hemessen's white headpiece contrasts with the dark background, thus drawing attention to the serious expression on her face. She grasps many paintbrushes and a full palette of paint in her left hand, alluding to the elaborateness of what she is about to render and master.

Italian Renaissance painter Sofonisba Anguissola channeled a similar theme in her *Self Portrait* from 1556. Known by art historians as the first female artist to master a "man's profession," Anguissola managed to evade much of the scrutiny that her male contemporaries exercised on her female successors.[220] Aside from talent, her appealing physical appearance contributed to her success, as contemporaries would have understood her self-portraits to be incarnations of works created by a female and personifications of their creator's beauty (female beauty having been a metaphor for the art of painting).[221] These characteristics also exemplified the woman of court, as outlined by Italian courtier, soldier, diplomat, and author Baldassare Castiglione in his *Book of the Courtier* from 1528:

---

[217] Ibid.
[218] James A. Welu and Pieter Biesboer, *Judith Leyster: A Dutch Master and Her World* (Worcester: Waanders Printers, Zwolle, 1993), 165.
[219] Nancy G. Heller, *Women Artists: An Illustrated History* (New York: Abbeville Press, 1997), 24.
[220] Joanna Woods-Marsden, *Renaissance Self-Portraiture* (New Haven and London: Yale University Press, 1998), 191. For further study, see Michael W. Cole, *Sofonisba's Lesson: A Renaissance Artist and Her Work* (Princeton, New Jersey: Princeton University Press, 2020); Leticia Ruiz Gómez, *A Tale of Two Women Painters: Sofonisba Anguissola and Lavinia Fontana* (Madrid: Museo Nacional del Prado, 2019).
[221] Ibid, 192.

I wish this [Court] Lady to have knowledge of letters, music, painting, and to know how to dance and make merry; accompanying the other precepts that have been taught the Courtier with discreet modesty and with the giving of a good impression of herself. And thus, in her talk, her laughter, her play, her jesting, in short, in everything, she will be very graceful, and will entertain appropriately, and with witticisms and pleasantries befitting her, everyone who shall come before her.[222]

Operating within a sphere in which she was deprived of extensive rigorous training and reliant upon inherent talent and beauty, Anguissola was also restricted to private commissions (public works such as altarpieces and other forms of large-scale history paintings were reserved for males), as well as to the inferior genre of portraiture.[223] As Leyster would do a century later, Anguissola prospered within these restrictive realms to overcome her boundaries. As has been stated earlier, portraiture was considered an appropriate domain for women painters since their hypothetical intellectual subordination barred them from other genres. Unlike Leyster, however, Anguissola was born into an aristocratic family. As such, she had the privilege of utilizing her lineage and subsequently portrayed herself as a courtly, high-class individual, simultaneously exhibiting her talent and qualifications to be a female painter and resident at court.[224] On account of her social class and artistic talents, King Philip II invited the artist to join the household of his French bride, Isabel of Valois.[225] Along with her career trajectory, Anguissola's study of expressive facial features and resolution of portraiture into genre scenes comprised her singularity as an artist, as will be shown and compared with Leyster's artistic characteristics.[226]

Anguissola's *Self Portrait* (fig. 20) perfectly exemplifies the artist's creative amalgamation of genres, anticipating Leyster's own self-portrait. Much like van Hemessen, she adopts a fixed gaze toward the observer and sits before an easel that faces the viewer. Even more

[222] James A. Welu and Pieter Biesboer, *Judith Leyster: A Dutch Master and Her World* (Worcester: Waanders Printers, Zwolle, 1993), 164; Baldassare Castiglione, *The Book of the Courtier*, translated by Leonard Eckstein Opdycke (New York: Charles Scribner's Sons, 1901), 180.
[223] Joanna Woods-Marsden, *Renaissance Self-Portraiture* (New Haven and London: Yale University Press, 1998), 192.
[224] Ibid, 193.
[225] Ibid, 195.
[226] Ibid, 196-7.

audaciously than van Hemessen, though, she looks directly out at the viewer (a display of self-assurance), and portrayed herself in the act of painting the Virgin and Child rather than awaiting artistic inspiration.[227] Earlier in this study, the hierarchy of painting genres was delineated, whereby history paintings, which included both secular and religious scenes, were placed at the top of the hierarchy due to their superior display value and ability to convey morals. By portraying herself painting a religious scene, Anguissola metaphorically raised her own standing to that of a sophisticated artist capable of rivaling her Old Master male predecessors and contemporaries. Since this gambit is contained within a self-portrait, the self-portrait is, by extension, elevated to the status of religious painting. The clarity and detail with which Anguissola painted the composition, as well as the urbane clothing that she lent herself, echo her preeminent standing and signify diffidence. A ruffled collar comprises the refined outfit which, in conjunction with the presence of chiaroscuro, draws viewers' eyes to the artist's striking countenance. Likewise, the gesture of the Virgin in the painting within the self-portrait, in which she draws the face of Christ close to her own while peering deeply into his eyes, reiterates the intensity and penetrative quality of the artist's gaze.

During an era in which men were regarded as creative facilitators and women as passive objects, Anguissola reversed these roles and presented herself as the creative force in charge of a passive, inanimate art object.[228] Giorgio Vasari, an Italian painter, architect, writer, and historian, affirmed this role reversal in his *Lives of the Artists* from 1550:

> But Sofonisba of Cremona, the daughter of Messer Amilcaro Anguisciuola, has worked with deeper study and greater grace than any other woman of our times at problems of design, for not only has she learned to draw, paint, and copy from nature, and reproduce most skillfully works by other artists, but she has on her own painted some most rare and beautiful paintings. Thus, it was well deserved when Philip, King of Spain, having heard about her talents and merits from the Duke of Alba, sent for her and had her brought with the greatest honor to Spain, where he supports her in the queen's company

---

[227] James A. Welu and Pieter Biesboer, *Judith Leyster: A Dutch Master and Her World* (Worcester: Waanders Printers, Zwolle, 1993), 164.

[228] Mary Garrard, "Here's Looking at Me: Sofonisba Anguissola and the Problem of the Woman Artist," *Renaissance Quarterly* 47 (1994): 556.

with a huge provision, to the amazement of all his court which admires as a wondrous thing Sophonisba's excellence.[229]

To be acknowledged by Vasari was no small feat, for he was the first great Italian art historian and wrote of only the most distinguished artists.[230] In light of this exceptional praise, the experimentation that Anguissola employed in her *Self Portrait with Bernardino Campi* from 1559 (fig. 21) takes on even greater significance. Campi, one of Anguissola's instructors, is shown delicately depicting his pupil on a stately canvas. Both he and his subject look out at the viewer, imploring him or her to unveil and deconstruct the layers of visual intricacy at play here. The scene is arranged as if Anguissola was in the middle of being painted by her instructor and the viewer has interrupted an important, candid moment. The layers are not only elaborate, but also methodically and adeptly executed. Chiaroscuro illuminates the figures' faces and the impeccable detailing of each feature. Ornamentation on Anguissola's vibrant clothing shimmers, indicating movement, spontaneity, and a palpable presence. A white lace collar further draws attention to her face. To transition from a microcosmic to a macrocosmic perspective, the scale of Anguissola's figure is noticeably larger, higher, and more centrally-placed than that of her teacher.[231] Consequently, a visual hierarchy is constructed which implies that, after learning from Campi, Anguissola blossomed into a painter in her own right. In fact, she burgeoned to such a high degree that, rather than painting Campi, he is now painting her (or, more accurately, she is painting him painting her).

A more omnipresent element that extends past the borders of the canvas is the invisible Anguissola who dictates the entire scene as the artist of the invention. Both Campi and the painted Anguissola look up at this ethereal larger presence outside of the canvas, implying that

---

[229] Giorgio Vasari, *The Lives of the Artists* (New York: Oxford University Press, 2008), 343.
[230] Fredrika H. Jacobs, "Woman's Capacity to Create: The Unusual Case of Sofonisba Anguissola," *Renaissance Quarterly* 47 (1994): 93.
[231] Mary Garrard, "Here's Looking at Me: Sofonisba Anguissola and the Problem of the Woman Artist," *Renaissance Quarterly* 47 (1994): 562.

her perspective comprises the whole work.[232] In addition to being physically and figuratively larger, the painted Anguissola is also strategically placed within the composition. The canvas containing her image is aligned with the painting's central axis and appears taller than Campi, making Anguissola equally as present as her male teacher.[233] In light of Anguissola's extant presence, Campi's talents seem to pale in comparison. His painting of Anguissola is static compared to her "living" rendering of him, and he grasps a *mahlstick*, an artist's tool to steady the hand which signifies the need of support, or weakness.[234] In brief, this self-portrait testifies to Anguissola's incredible ingenuity and to the inventiveness that female painters honed when relegated to only one painting category.

If Anguissola's *Self Portrait* was a clever construction, Leyster took originality several steps further in her *Self Portrait* from 1635. The artist, like the women artists before her, gazes out at the viewer while manipulating a canvas that faces the observer. Also akin to her predecessors, she wears not the clothes of a painter, but rather those of a cultured and refined woman.[235] Nevertheless, in lieu of the stiff, closed-mouthed poses discernable in both male and female self-portraits at easels, Leyster laughs and leans back in her chair. The open-mouthed smile signifies merriment, movement, and Leyster's intent to make a literal and metaphorical statement as to her place in the contemporary art world.[236] That place was as an accomplished painter capable of competing with male colleagues.

James Welu and Pieter Biesboer have suggested that so great is Leyster's confidence in her artistic craft that she unabashedly exudes ease and relaxation and transfers this mood to her canvas.[237] More specifically, though she reveals her easel to viewers in the same manner as her

---

[232] Ibid.
[233] Ibid.
[234] Ibid, 562, 564.
[235] James A. Welu and Pieter Biesboer, *Judith Leyster: A Dutch Master and Her World* (Worcester: Waanders Printers, Zwolle, 1993), 162.
[236] Ibid.
[237] Ibid.

female predecessors, she strays from a blank canvas, as we saw with van Hemessen, or a traditional religious or historical scene or even a double portrait, as with Anguissola. Instead, Leyster depicts a jovial musician whose own open mouth and casual stance mirror her pose and attests to her ability to capture the natural emotion of men and women.[238] Additionally, by painting a jolly figure who recalls the bawdiness of genre scenes, Leyster nodded to her ability to surpass the gender confines of the hierarchy of genres.

Both Leyster and the musician look outward to invite the viewer to participate in the spontaneity. This double gaze, though reminiscent of the one in *Self Portrait with Bernardino Campi*, is starkly different from Anguissola's. Whereas Anguissola's self-portrait looks out at the viewer as the object of a male painter (notwithstanding Anguissola having painted herself larger, higher, and more centrally-situated than her teacher), Leyster looks out at the viewer as the creator of a painting containing a male figure, thus poignantly taking the artist-object and male-female role reversals to an even greater level. As a result of the double gaze and jovial atmosphere in Leyster's work, the self-portrait is transformed into an engaging genre scene that captures a cheerful moment in time. In the process, Leyster's ability to re-define the possibilities of portraiture and expression is affirmed. Rather than incorporate a history scene on her canvas, as Anguissola did, or include status-raising worldly objects, as Claesz had, Leyster's mere adroit rendering of the figures' confidence and mastery of expression were enough to place genre scenes on the same pedestal as portraiture, and to endeavor to place her status as an artist on the same pillar as those of her art market competition, both male and female alike. The preceding chapter has focused on Leyster's self-portrait in order to underline the novel ways in which she challenged traditional representations of expression in portraiture. The next two chapters will now turn to Leyster's portraits of children and animals in order to consider how these unique representations of expression aided in preserving a sense of innocence. To fulfill

---

[238] Ibid, 165.

this objective, the following chapters, akin to this one, shall comparatively examine other artists' works from earlier and contemporary periods.

Chapter 3: Leyster's Self Portrait in Comparison with her Own Paintings of Children

The unique qualities of Leyster's *Self Portrait* carried over into her paintings of children. Accordingly, the former and latter works shall be compared with one another. Before delving into these comparisons, though, an examination of an earlier painting of a child will help to frame the typical characteristics of earlier portraits of children, thereby further highlighting how Leyster's works departed from the others'. An example of an exceptional portrait of a child prior to Leyster's career, and one that devotes equal attention to detail as Leyster's works, is Titian's *Portrait of Clarissa Strozzi* from 1542 (fig. 22). The youngest of seven daughters born to prominent Florentine patrician Roberto Strozzi and Maddalena de Medici, Clarissa was the only Strozzi child to be painted at this time or in this fashion.[239] In the portrait, the round-cheeked, golden-curled, brown-eyed Clarissa stands in the center of the picture plane, her full-length figure comprising nearly the entire composition.[240] While holding a white lap-dog in her left hand and feeding it with a ring-shaped roll that she grasps in the other, Clarissa appears to be interrupted by the spectator as she quickly looks outward and, like a fidgety child, turns her body as if in the process of shifting her stance in the composition.[241] This sense of vivid movement, along with Clarissa's cherubic features and tousled hair, serve to reinforce the girl's childlike vigor. The date stamp located above and to the left of Clarissa (Annor II MDXLII, or

---

[239] Laurel Reed, "Art, Life, Charm, and Titian's Portrait of Clarissa Strozzi" in Albrecht Classen, *Childhood in the Middle Ages and the Renaissance: The Results of a Paradigm Shift in the History of Mentality* (Berlin: De Gruyter, 2005), 363.
[240] Luba Freedman, "Titian's Portrait of Clarissa Strozzi: The State Portrait of a Child," *Jahrbuch der Berliner Museen* 31 (1989): 167.
[241] Laurel Reed, "Art, Life, Charm, and Titian's Portrait of Clarissa Strozzi" in Albrecht Classen, *Childhood in the Middle Ages and the Renaissance: The Results of a Paradigm Shift in the History of Mentality* (Berlin: De Gruyter, 2005), 362.

two years old in the year 1542) also serves to emphasize her childhood in the here and now.[242]

On her right wrist is a pearl bracelet that matches her pearl collar.[243] Her jewelry, along with her white satin dress, gold chain girdle that ends in a filigreed golden ball encrusted with precious stones, and white embroidered slipper, indicate that she is heiress to the most rich and gallant family of Florence.[244] The lap-dog sits atop a pedestal featuring a classical high relief sculpture of two dancing putti that is partially covered by flowing red velvet drapery.[245] Surrounding the full-length Clarissa and her dog are the walls of a room and a window that reveals the view of a pond with a pair of swans in the midst of a dense forest.[246] Clarissa's playful, angelic, and round figure, along with the feeding of the dog, the festiveness of the setting, and the white swans in the background that some scholars have identified as standing for her purity, were qualities unique to official, aristocratic portraits of children during the mid-Cinquecento.[247] Even her full-length, awkward contrapposto posture was unusual, as it would normally have been reserved for a subject of high social ranking who had a list of public achievements.[248] Equally unusual was the placement of her head before a window, as this positioning would have been reserved for a seated individual with worldly, exterior accomplishments.[249] Two-year-old Clarissa, of course, was a young girl with no such achievements. Rather than prefigure adult deeds, her posture seems to underscore her circular, childlike proportions.[250]

One element her body language did predict, however, was her potential to acquire the refinement needed to transition from a graceless, unlettered child to a graceful adult and ideal

---

[242] Maria Loh, *Titian's Touch: Art, Magic and Philosophy* (United Kingdom: Reaktion Books, 2019), 118.
[243] Luba Freedman, "Titian's Portrait of Clarissa Strozzi: The State Portrait of a Child," *Jahrbuch der Berliner Museen* 31 (1989): 167.
[244] Ibid.
[245] Ibid.
[246] Ibid.
[247] Ibid, 167-8.
[248] Ibid, 169.
[249] Brian D. Steele, "Titian's Clarissa Strozzi: The Infant as Ideal Bride" in Matthew Knox Averett's *The Early Modern Child in Art and History* (Philadelphia: Taylor & Francis, 2015), 155.
[250] Luba Freedman, "Titian's Portrait of Clarissa Strozzi: The State Portrait of a Child," *Jahrbuch der Berliner Museen* 31 (1989): 169.

wife.[251] Her white satin dress, pearls, gems, and the gold chain girdle that encircles and restrains her torso are evidently fitting at their maximum capacities, indicating that Clarissa will physically and figuratively transcend these clothes.[252] Akin to her pet and underscored by the sculptural relief of putti wrestling in the lower right-hand corner, Clarissa is tranquil and attentive but expected to experience bouts of feistiness and insolence given her age.[253] She will, of course, outgrow this phase and behave appropriately, as the aforesaid "coming-to-be" references are indisputably deliberate and aid in explaining the purpose of the portrait's commissioning.[254] Moreover, she is the personification of a dichotomy; a celebration of both her present unrefined state and the poise that is to come.[255] For Titian, this encapsulation in the figure of Clarissa was a chance to contend with the world in motion, arrest the ephemeral nature of childhood through an adult lens, and unite being (Clarissa in the moment of girlhood) with becoming (Clarissa on the horizon of maturity).[256] This type of visual record of the transient stage between infancy and adulthood was considered a distinctive and precious keepsake beginning in the mid- to late-Cinquecento.[257]

Leyster likely knew of Titian's art even if she had not seen this particular portrait. She did, nevertheless, possess the same skill of observation as the Italian painter. As will be shown in the following pages, Leyster, in her portraits of children, retained the same innocent and playful qualities that Titian bestowed upon Clarissa and explored the same balance between being and becoming, but without adhering to any single pictorial formula conventional to aristocratic

[251] Laurel Reed, "Art, Life, Charm, and Titian's Portrait of Clarissa Strozzi" in Albrecht Classen, *Childhood in the Middle Ages and the Renaissance: The Results of a Paradigm Shift in the History of Mentality* (Berlin: De Gruyter, 2005), 368; Maria Loh, *Titian's Touch: Art, Magic and Philosophy* (United Kingdom: Reaktion Books, 2019), 118.
[252] Maria Loh, *Titian's Touch: Art, Magic and Philosophy* (United Kingdom: Reaktion Books, 2019), 118-119.
[253] Ibid, 119.
[254] Laurel Reed, "Art, Life, Charm, and Titian's Portrait of Clarissa Strozzi" in Albrecht Classen, *Childhood in the Middle Ages and the Renaissance: The Results of a Paradigm Shift in the History of Mentality* (Berlin: De Gruyter, 2005), 368-69.
[255] Ibid, 369.
[256] Maria Loh, *Titian's Touch: Art, Magic and Philosophy* (United Kingdom: Reaktion Books, 2019), 119.
[257] Caroline P. Murphy, *Lavinia Fontana: A Painter and her Patrons in Sixteenth-century Bologna* (New Haven and London: Yale University Press, 2003), 175.

portraits of children. The theme of being on the cusp of tolerable and deplorable behavior is presented in Leyster's works where she portrays children engaging in mischievous acts while still retaining the appropriate innocence given their ages. Through explorations of expression and amalgamations of contrasting generic elements, Leyster's works reassessed, and surpassed the limitations of, standard painting types and traditional depictions of children.

LEYSTER'S SMILING GIRL

One such work is her *Girl with a Straw Hat* from 1635 (fig. 2), in which the young female subject has been interpreted to be dressed in the clothes of a shepherdess.[258] Shepherd and shepherdess themes were in vogue among aristocratic and patrician circles in The Hague, Utrecht, and Amsterdam from the 1620s through the end of the seventeenth century.[259] By the late 1620s and early 1630s, the themes expanded beyond these geographical areas and entered the mainstream art market.[260] Other artists' depictions of the shepherdess theme will first be explicated so as to place greater emphasis on Leyster's original interpretation of the subject. A conventional painting of the theme is exemplified in Salomon de Bray's *Shepherdess* from 1635 (fig. 23). A young woman in a bust-length pose occupies the composition as she stares out at the viewer. Her wide-brimmed straw hat dominates the upper half of the scene and identifies her as a shepherdess or someone posing as one; in her right hand she holds a cluster of plums, which are intended to be offered as a gift. As suggested by her plunging neckline, however, to which the plums seem to strategically point, the gift possesses erotic undertones.[261] It would seem that the purpose of the figure's shepherdess costume is to act as a vehicle to relay a sexual advance towards the viewer. If de Bray's girl is seductive, children could also parody adulthood. In

---

[258] James A. Welu and Pieter Biesboer, *Judith Leyster: A Dutch Master and Her World* (Worcester: Waanders Printers, Zwolle, 1993), 194.
[259] Ibid.
[260] Ibid.
[261] Ibid.

Molenaer's *Children Making Music* from the 1630s (fig. 24), all the children display mature poses and wear hats while partaking in adult pastimes. By sporting comically oversized hats, the children adopt the role of satirizing, mimicking, and poking fun at the adult roles they emulate. This, in turn, becomes the children's primary function.

In contrast to de Bray and Molenaer, the girl in Leyster's painting, although dressed as an adult who imitates a shepherdess, conveys neither the erotic undertones that are often present in shepherdess paintings nor the comedic aspect in images of children emulating adults.[262] The girl turns her head to her left side, her eyes cast downward. She wears clothes that an adult imitating a shepherdess would don.[263] Put simply, she is a child "all dressed up." Her white bib and large straw hat frame her face and direct the viewer's focus to her shiny and wavy hair. The wispy strands of her tangled hair (which were produced by scratching into wet paint), along with free-handled brushstrokes and the play of light and shadow, imbue the portrait with spontaneity, vivacity, and animation, all of which also serve to remind viewers that she is not an adult.[264] Instead, she is a child pretending to be an adult pretending to be a shepherdess. Her tousled hair, slight grin, turned head, and downcast eyes suggest the coyness and mischievousness of a clever child.[265] Yet at the same time, there is a pensiveness and reflectiveness in her sideways glance that is reminiscent of an adult. Unlike de Bray's and Molenaer's children, her adult-like qualities contain no suggestive undertones, and the bust-length mode leaves no room for a mature physical stance or any reference to her future adult self. In addition to cropping any trace of the girl's imminent adulthood, the composition also implores viewers to focus on her face and its emotional subtleties, particularly the slight asymmetry of her facial features that lends her smile its playfulness. In sum, the girl is dressed

---

[262] Ibid.
[263] Ibid.
[264] Ibid; Frima Fox Hofrichter, *Judith Leyster, 1609–1660* (Washington, DC: National Gallery of Art, 2009), 14.
[265] James A. Welu and Pieter Biesboer, *Judith Leyster: A Dutch Master and Her World* (Worcester: Waanders Printers, Zwolle, 1993), 194.

as an adult but maintains her youthful coyness and innocence, making her an intriguing study of expression.

Both finished in 1635, Leyster's *Girl with a Straw Hat* and *Self Portrait* share much more in common than their year of completion. Despite the former being a painting of a child and the latter a painting of the adult artist, each work defied traditions using similar unconventional elements of expression. Akin to the ruffled collar that draws attention to Leyster's face, the straw hat worn by the young girl leads viewers' eyes to her tousled hair, which in turn draws attention to her delicate features. A bright white bib frames her face in much the same way as Leyster's collar as well. Cropped as such, these poses ensure and reinforce the efficaciousness of these framing elements. Though understated and with her eyes slightly cast downward and to the side, a smile plays across the girl's face. This contrasts with that of Leyster's bold hearty smile, which is coupled with welcoming eyes that are fixed on the viewer. If the one female figure is being puckish and the other brazen, each smile breaks from longstanding traditions.

Leyster's charming smile contrasts with the staid countenances typically used in portraits and self-portraits, imparting instead an air of self-composure not commonly seen in portraits of women. Likewise, the girl's smile retains the figure's innocence, a feature that is often absent from shepherdess paintings and images of children imitating adults which tend to contain amatory connotations. The mischievousness of the girl's smile also recalls the playfulness of the laughing musician on Leyster's canvas, thus exhibiting the range of distinct and original methods that Leyster developed to convey similar spirited, childlike qualities. Altogether, the spontaneity and liveliness of the figures in each work are matched and enhanced by painterly, animated brushstrokes that comprise the ruffled collar and wispy strands of hair. Though composed of soft, loosely-applied brush strokes, the facial features of Leyster and the shepherdess girl are nonetheless highly detailed.

56

Other paintings of children by Leyster take the exploration of expression to a more vivacious level than *Girl with a Straw Hat*, and do more to transition away from portraiture and enter into the realm of genre scenes. Anguissola once again foreshadowed Leyster's approach to her blended portrayals of children in her *Boy Bitten by a Crawfish* from 1554 (fig. 25). In his *Lives of the Artist*, Vasari showers this work and Anguissola's abilities with tremendous applause, noting Michelangelo's praise of the drawing:

> Not long ago Messer Tommaso Cavalieri, a Roman gentleman, sent to Lord Duke Cosimo, in addition to a drawing by the divine Michelangelo which contains a Cleopatra, another drawing by Sophonisba, in which a young girl is laughing at a small boy crying, because after she had placed a basket full of lobsters in front of him, one of them bit his finger. One could not see a more graceful or realistic drawing than this one. Since she lives in Spain and Italy does not possess copies of her works, I have placed it in our sketchbook in memory of Sophonisba's talent.[266]

Noted in Cavalieri's description of Anguissola's work, a boy winces in pain after being bitten by a crawfish while a young girl attends to him on his left side. The half-length mode draws significant attention to the immensely heightened, beguiling expression on the boy's face. The boy looks out towards the viewer as if to make sure that his distress is being made known. One can almost hear the boy crying due to the precise detailing in his scrunched features and in the use of vigorous lines to define his surprised and pained facial expression. These lines, along with the realistic detailing (noted by Vasari), cropped edges, and feeling of incursion by the viewer, transform the drawing into a transitory moment that has been brilliantly captured. By being a snapshot in time in which all three figures (the boy, the girl, and the viewer) are in conversation with one another, the work recalls the anecdotal, trifling, and everyday moments that would

---

[266] Giorgio Vasari, *The Lives of the Artists* (New York: Oxford University Press, 2008), 343.

occur later in seventeenth-century domestic genre scenes.[267] Since these moments are rarely isolated or not part of a larger narrative, one could almost envisage Anguissola's crying boy as being one of many elements going awry as a maternal figure tries to subdue a rowdy household.[268]

Leyster rendered her own intensely expressive and amusing boy in *A Card Player* from 1630 (fig. 3). Although the painting contains the same childlike innocence that is extant in *Girl with a Straw Hat*, the boy's dynamic expressiveness is more befitting to the types of characters that we would find in a genre scene. In this work, a young boy points to a deck of playing cards that are fanned out in his left hand and held by endearingly plump fingers. He wears clothing that fails to suit his youthfully rotund body and a feathered hat so large that it droops over his left eye. Although the clothing parodies those of an adult, they manage to retain the child's playfulness due to their laughably oversized, ill-fitting quality. Owing to the cropped nature of the half-length composition, the clothing, and in particular the feather, also act as a framing mechanism for the boy's laughing face. Arched in a half-circle or crescent formation, the feather tosses the viewer's eye back and forth between the deck of playing cards and the boy's silly expression. Distracted by an occurrence taking place beyond the picture plane, the boy looks to his left and appears to be on the verge of moving his body and hand in response to the external event upon which he is fixated, lending the work a sense of presence and the feeling of continuous motion all at once. This dynamism, in conjunction with swift, lively brushstrokes, especially in the rendering of the feather, converts the work from a straightforward portrait of a child to a capturing of an ephemeral moment that is reminiscent of those in genre scenes.

This shift from portraiture to genre scene evokes the ebullient musician in Leyster's *Self Portrait*. Like the boy in *A Card Player*, and akin to the female artist who has brought him into being, the musician, too, smiles open-mouthed, wears cheerful, floppy clothing, and appears to

---

[267] William Henry Goodyear, *Renaissance and Modern Art* (New York: Flood & Vincent, 1894), 191.
[268] Ibid, 193.

be on the brink of movement. One imagines that he is lifting his hand to play a chord on the violin and shifting the weight in his legs in response to the rhythmic notes. The musician looks out at the viewer along with Leyster as he prepares to translate his energy from potential to kinetic, engendering direct viewer engagement and crossing the threshold into genre painting. Metaphorically speaking, the card-playing boy may be considered a prefiguration of the cheery musician. Whereas the boy's silly grin, plump frame, and painterly brushstrokes reinforce the fact that he is an innocent child (despite his adult costume); the musician, meanwhile, is an adult who, through his previously-described expression, costume, gestures, and swift brushstrokes, channels a pure, childlike essence that is not unlike that of the card-playing boy. Together, each figure exhibits Leyster's confident ability to waver between childlike innocence and maturity, and between portraiture and genre scenes. Finally, the playing card that the boy holds is akin to the canvas within Leyster's self-portrait. Both are presented to the viewer as flat surfaces while doubling as illusions. The one is a playing card and the other a painting; both are images within images, clever visual puns in each work.

To summarize, this chapter analyzed the ways in which Leyster's innovative use of expression to preserve innocence in paintings of children separated her works from more traditional renderings of children. Additionally, it looked at the ways in which her paintings of children connected to her self-portrait and blurred the line between portraitures and genre painting. As will be elucidated in the final chapter, Leyster's paintings of children more fully enter the genre scene category when figures as expressive as the card-playing boy are juxtaposed with additional children and animals, and references to proverbs are integrated into the works.

Chapter 4: Leyster's Paintings of Children and Animals in Comparison to Earlier and Contemporary Artists' Paintings of Children and Animals

By the late seventeenth century, the convergence of genre painting and portraiture became a common trait in Dutch naturalism.[269] More specifically, as David Smith has outlined, genre scenes often simulated the characteristics of portraiture, thereby indicating Dutch artists' cognizance of the role of standard limitations in the prescribed terms of naturalism, as well as the extent to which portrait characteristics were directly associated with social customs of courtesy and modesty.[270] Smith based his conclusion on the examination of several paintings, including Eglon Hendrik Van der Neer's *Couple in an Interior* from approximately 1675 (fig. 26).[271] At first glance, the painting is a straightforward portrait in which a wealthy couple is surrounded by luxurious wares reflective of a comfortable middle-class Dutch lifestyle.[272] However, a routine cleaning in 1963 revealed that the landscape hanging above the couple's fireplace was actually thinly-veiling an image of Venus and Cupid.[273] Despite the theme's associations with love, beauty, and faithfulness, the image would have been a conspicuous anomaly in a Dutch marriage portrait, therefore rendering the work simultaneously a genre scene.[274] In an attempt to turn the painting into a straightforward portrait, the Venus and Cupid image was subsequently hidden by a landscape.[275]

---

[269] David R. Smith, "Irony and Civility: Notes on the Convergence of Genre and Portraiture in Seventeenth-Century Dutch Painting," *The Art Bulletin* 69 (September 1987): 407, 410.
[270] Ibid, 407-408.
[271] Ibid, 411.
[272] Ibid.
[273] Ibid.
[274] Ibid.
[275] Ibid.

In contrast to Smith's thesis, which argues that genre scenes came to be excluded from portraiture, this chapter will demonstrate how Leyster's portraits of children and animals, painted at the end of the seventeenth century, adopted the characteristics of genre scenes, or rather, how they blurred the boundary between the two.

Often, scenes of children interacting with animals are obvious incarnations of adult witticisms and proverbs, such as in *Child with a Cat* by Cornelis Bloemaert, a print made after a painting by his brother, Hendrick Bloemaert, from 1625 (fig. 27). Initially trained as a painter by his father, Abraham, along with his brothers, Hendrick and Adriaan, Cornelis dedicated himself predominantly to printmaking, which he learned from Dutch publisher and engraver Crispihn van de Passe.[276] Hendrick painted a number of works in which adults were shown with children. Interestingly, Cornelis depicted similar subjects in a series of prints, yet featured children with animals in lieu of adults with children.

From the visual evidence, it would seem that the print medium allowed for greater frivolity. Such expression is present in *Child with a Cat*. In it, a boy gazes out at the viewer while holding a black-and-white cat between both arms. The sleeve on his left shoulder has fallen, exposing his shoulder, throat, and most of his chest. The fallen sleeve dares the viewer to stare, perhaps even touch, the boy's barren flesh. This sensual persona echoes the inscription written on the bottom of the print, which reads, "You like birds; I prefer cats/ But, friend, watch out that they don't catch you."[277] Deciphered in plainer terms, the inscription implies that cats stalk birds, as boys chase girls.[278] Cats, such as the one the boy holds, were known metaphors for

---

[276] Arnold Houbraken, *De groote schouburgh der Nederlantsche konstschilders en schilderessen* (Digital Library for Dutch Literature, 1718).
[277] Cornelis Bloemaert translated by James A. Welu and Pieter Biesboer in *Judith Leyster: A Dutch Master and Her World* (Worcester: Waanders Printers, Zwolle, 1993), 138.
[278] Ibid.

erotic desire in seventeenth-century Dutch art due to their primitive hunting and preying instincts.[279]

According to some, one of the greatest influences of the Netherlands on European erotic culture during the seventeenth century was the depiction of lewd subjects and subtly thrilling ones in large numbers of genre paintings and religious, political, cityscape, and portrait prints of extremely high illustrative quality and complexity.[280] *Child with a Cat* contains specific sexual references in which the boy, akin to the predatory cat he is holding and as evidenced by his fallen sleeve, is figured as a future girl chaser and pursuer of forbidden desires. He sports tousled hair and a youthful countenance and is invigorated by animated lines. He drifts between childhood and adulthood, but the inscription in the print places him closer to the latter. The cat seems to be cognizant of his dormant pursuit of pleasures by way of the intensity of its expression. Although the boy may be too young to fully realize his mature potential, the cat looks fixedly out at the viewer as if to acknowledge its existence. Furthermore, in contrast to Leyster's card-playing boy, who is carefree and jolly, Bloemaert's boy is sexualized; like de Bray's young shepherdess, they appear mature beyond their years.

Aside from exuding sensual connotations, children and animals were used as vehicles in themes of morality as well, such as the hazards of excessive imbibing, pictured in Jan Steen's genre scene *The Effects of Intemperance* from 1663-65 (fig. 28). Painted some years after Leyster's death, we see a shared interest in the study of expression, namely those of children shifting between age-appropriate and adult roles. This work, as will be explicated, also introduces the compositional device of showing multiple children, and hence multiple expressions, in conversation with one another. In the foreground of the scene, two women

[279] Wayne E. Franits, *From Revolt to Riches: Culture and History of the Low Countries, 1500–1700* (United Kingdom: UCL Press, 2017), 220.
[280] Nadine M. Orenstein, "Stepping Up to the Plate: The State of Research in Seventeenth-Century Dutch Prints" in Wayne E. Franits' *The Ashgate Research Companion to Dutch Painting* (London and New York: Routledge, 2016), 311.

(presumably the mothers, nursemaids, and/or guardians of the children) have succumbed to the effects of alcohol. One falls asleep on the stoop, her face tucked onto her left arm as she slumps over and loses the grip of the object in her right hand, the anticipation of its fall adding tension to the scene of "lowly" characters. In front of her, another woman crawls on her knees and musters just enough energy to address a parrot sitting on a perch. She looks at it quizzically, feeding it wine from a glass as she does so. To her left, a jug has tipped over and grapes and what appears to be bread are strewn about the ground. Bread, or humility and the body of Christ, have been abandoned for the Bacchanalian fruit. A seated couple in the background contrasts with the women's behavior, and a pig between the two women sniffs an object on the ground that should probably not be within its reach.

Although the women are the focus of the composition with their pastel-colored clothing and deep, shining drapery folds, the children in the middle ground play pivotal roles. With the grown women incapacitated, the children are now the "adults" as they are left to fend for themselves. Despite being in charge, however, they are but children after all, and continue to act their ages, lampooning the adults' behavior and initiating mischief. One child, likely the youngest, peers behind the slumped woman and gazes at her suspiciously, unsure as to the circumstances of the scene and if he/she now has the freedom to sneak away. A boy stands behind the pig and appears to tease it and make jeering noises to attract its attention. Additionally, a group of three children stand behind the woman feeding the parrot and proceed to mock her behavior. More specifically, a girl looks on in fascination as a boy holds a cat while another girl feeds it table scraps or human food, just as the woman does with the parrot.

All the children, particularly the group of three, wear adult clothing and are shown in a full-length mode that reveals adult poses. Furthermore, they function as moralizing vehicles to transmit the adult message not to overindulge in pleasures such as alcohol, and are intended to be interpreted as miniature or microcosmic adults. The boy holding the cat turns and flashes the audience an enormous open-mouthed smile, starkly contrasting with the engrossed expressions of the rest of the children to let the viewer in on his secret that he is completely cognizant of what is occurring. This direct inclusion of the viewer, combined with the rowdy atmosphere and demonstration of a moral teaching, make for a quintessential genre scene and exhibit an archetypal portrayal of children and animals in Dutch seventeenth-century paintings of this category.

When not conveying sensual undercurrents or relaying lessons in morality, children with animals were also shown as people acting their ages, a concept perfectly exemplified by the theme of children impersonating adults while giving instructions to household pets as if they were offspring, consequently tormenting them (often times intentionally under the guise of play).[281] Steen's *The Effects of Intemperance* depicts children in the midst of childhood as well, but the work contains moral undercurrents that are assuaged or more latent in the paintings discussed in the following pages.

CHILDREN BEING CHILDREN

Anguissola's *Boy Bitten by a Crawfish* again serves as an ideal precursor to this subcategory of children and animals in genre scenes. Previously described as an expressive snapshot in time in which the boy, the girl, and the viewer are in conversation with one another, recalling everyday occurrences that would become common in seventeenth-century Dutch domestic genre scenes, Anguissola's drawing also shows the result of children engaging in age-appropriate mischief. The boy has somehow come in close enough contact with a crawfish to be bitten by it while the girl beside him smiles, either because she contributed to his being bitten and/or views the boy's reaction as being ill-fitting for an otherwise insignificant injury or as just

---

[281] James A. Welu and Pieter Biesboer, *Judith Leyster: A Dutch Master and Her World* (Worcester: Waanders Printers, Zwolle, 1993), 200.

punishment for his mischief. Either way, the children have involved a creature (and the upsetting of it) in their antics. Unlike Bloemaert and Steen but similar to Leyster's juvenile figures, Anguissola's sister and brother are without the presence of erotic references. They are simply children acting their ages while also serving as a study of sudden, fleeting expression.

Much like *Boy Bitten by a Crawfish*, Annibale Carracci's *Two Children Teasing a Cat* from 1590 (fig. 29) depicts ill-behaved children acting their ages as they mock an animal for their own personal enjoyment, without suggestive connotations or overt lessons in morality. Unlike Anguissola's drawing, though, the boy's expression is milder, and the painting style (or the half-length mode in combination with the use of bright colors and subtle attention to detail) is more in line with that of Leyster's. A boy dangles a scorpion above a cat's ear, close enough for one of its pinchers to latch onto it. Another scorpion stands dangerously close to the cat's front paws. A girl to the boy's right watches the pincher clutch the cat's ear and places her left hand on his shoulder, gesturing for the boy to pay close attention and containing her fascination and excitement. Like the girl in Anguissola's drawing, her amused expression encourages the tormenting of an animal for the benefit of their gratification, despite the fact that she herself is not directly performing an action against the pet.

The half-length mode draws greater attention to the figures' detailed expressions, such as the boy's satisfied grin, the girl's wide-eyed, gaping smile of captivation, and the cat's winced eyes, arched back, and stiff posture as it endures the discomfort. Painterly brushstrokes animate the figures and the creases in their outfits caused by movement, amplifying the illusion of spontaneity and contributing to the work's overall placement in the genre scene category. The children are not parodying adults but are merely acting their ages, yet their innocence is tainted by their behavior at the animal's expense and the flagrant disregard for the cat's safety. By being at the mercy of the children, the cat is a mere curiosity piece and its presence and expression are subordinate to those of the children.

Steen painted several works with this theme of naughty children and unfortunate animals, including *Children Teaching a Cat to Read* from between 1665 and 1668 (fig. 30), *Children Teasing a Cat* from 1665 (fig. 31), *The Cat's Medicine* from 1663 (fig. 32), and *Children Teaching a Cat to Dance* from 1660-79 (fig. 33). For the sake of concision I will focus on this last image. *Children Teaching a Cat to Dance* depicts a boy balancing a cat on a kitchen table while lifting and stretching its front legs to create the appearance that it is dancing. A girl plays a flute in front of the cat so as to provide musical accompaniment for the "dance" and to incite the dog on the floor to menacingly bark at the cat. Two boys watch in delight, one of whom lifts his head back and howls with laughter (a compositional parallel to the dog). An elderly man peering in through a window above the table watches in horror and surprise as the uncivilized nature of the children unfolds. As such, a literal and metaphorical hierarchy of behavior is established, whereby the most civilized figures are on top and the least civilized (the animals) are on the bottom.

Ironically, however, the civilized humans (the children) are the ones behaving like animals as they inflict misery on the household pets. The cat is especially affected by the situation at hand, as evidenced by its squinted eyes and open mouth, which are indicative of hissing and meowing in discontentment. The children, particularly the boy who looks out at the viewer and laughs, derive sadistic pleasure from the animal's discomfort. Though they occupy a tavern-like environment and ridicule adults through their mature outfits (which include a ruffled collar, feathered hat, and elegant dress with deep drapery folds that fosters a play of light and shadow), the figures' immature behavior firmly consigns them to the realm of childhood. Nonetheless, their "civilized" status in the human-animal hierarchy is reduced to that of the pets by their uncivilized behavior, or the intentional ignoring of the cat's noticeable pain. This cruelness and maliciousness is justified by their act of childish play. In turn, this justification leads to the moral of the work, which is that humans can be more beastly than beasts, and children less innocent than adults (hence the inclusion of the disapproving old man in the window as a frame of reference).

EXPRESSIVE JOY IN LEYSTER'S PAINTINGS

In lieu of these profoundly moralizing lessons masking as genre scenes, Leyster upheld the expressive joy of childhood, provided animals with integral roles in her studies of expression, and imbued her paintings of children and animals with a joyfulness that is missing from those of her male peers. Her *Two Children with a Cat* from 1629 (fig. 4) is a fitting exemplification of this freshness.[282] Two boys occupy the entirety of the composition in which the older one withholds a treat from the cat in the clutches of his left hand while the younger one attempts to nab the cat. The cat is still uncomfortable in the boy's grip, yet the discomfort does not reduce the cat to a mere prop, plaything, or object of the boys' puerile antics. Instead, the image personifies the cat and provides the artist with a means for depicting a range of realistic expressions of the very kind that Le Brun sought to codify some decades later. In other words, Leyster devoted equal attention to the faces of the two boys and the cat and established her prowess at painting multiple expressions at once.

The older boy is dressed in the colorful, feathered, and eye-catching costume of a carnival reveler. While this costume may embody and satirize the role of an adult, its primary purpose is to frame the figure and lend further playfulness to the fun-loving, lighthearted genre scene comprised of a strong diagonal composition and rapid, activated brushstrokes.[283] The boys' tousled hair (analogous to that of the figure in *Girl with a Straw Hat*) contributes to this liveliness as well. Each rosy-cheeked boy dons a wide, toothy smile with an impish, rascally glint in their eyes. The younger one directs his naughty gaze towards the cat, while the older one

---

[282] Ibid, 136.
[283] Ibid.

peers directly out at the viewer, welcoming him or her into his puckish boyhood games. The cat, meanwhile, looks towards the viewer as well, with a humorously deadpan expression and huge pleading eyes that reflect its desire to be set free. Despite being teased, the cat is not being tortured, which assuages the cruelty existent in other images of children and animals. In this instance, the boys are truly acting their ages; they are children being children. In short, Leyster introduced thoughtfulness to the children-animal theme by undertaking a careful study of the cat's expression, too.

Additional layers of complexity are present in Leyster's *Two Children with a Cat and an Eel* from 1630 (fig. 5). A boy cradles a cat in his right arm and holds up an eel in his left, employing a Dutch proverb, "To hold an eel by the tail" (that is, just because a person has something does not mean that he or she can hold on to it).[284] Next to the boy, a girl pulls the cat's tail and lifts her right hand, pointing her index finger in a didactic manner that confirms the teaching and relaying of the proverb, as well as women's tendency to be portrayed as unstable as the holding of an eel's tail.[285] However, unlike Bloemaert's print and as prominent as the proverb seems, the children, house pet, and reptile's primary purpose is not to convey an explicit moral lesson about the "proper" place of girls and boys.[286] Rather, as will be made apparent, they are important first and foremost as an exploration of human emotion. The girl's expression is especially unusual, as her lined face and hunched posture resemble those of an elderly woman. She hovers between a child and an adult just as the work wavers between a portrait and a genre scene. Nevertheless, her flushed cheeks and playful grin negate her elderly qualities and are comparable to those of the boy. With an equally rosy complexion and toothy, coy smile, the boy darts his eyes upward at something beyond the border of the picture plane, transforming the portrait into a genre scene that captures a fleeting moment. As the boy looks

---

[284] Neil MacLaren and Christopher Brown, *Catalogue of the Dutch School, Vol. 2, 1600-1900* (Washington, D.C.: National Gallery, 1991), 227.
[285] James A. Welu and Pieter Biesboer, *Judith Leyster: A Dutch Master and Her World* (Worcester: Waanders Printers, Zwolle, 1993), 200.
[286] Ibid.

up and away from the viewer, feigning innocence while dangling the eel above the girl's head, the girl promptly wrests control of the scene by establishing a direct engagement with the viewer.[287]

Whereas in previous paintings of children with cats, boys are the impetus behind mischief and girls are simply onlookers, the roles have been cleverly reversed.[288] One might think back to the similar gender dynamic in Anguissola's self-portrait with Campi (fig. 21). The girl pulls the cat's tail, causing the boy to eventually and inevitably be scratched by the cat, and clues the viewer in on her surreptitious intent.[289] Not only does the girl look at the viewer, but the cat does so as well. Just as in *Two Children with a Cat*, the pet is not being tormented, but, judging by its piercing eyes that signal to the viewer for help, it is not thrilled to be in the boy's arm or to have its tailed pulled, either. Moreover, rather than demote the animal to a mere object, the cat's annoyance anthropomorphizes it and provides it with an outlet for its expressiveness to be showcased. Again, the image highlights Leyster's capacity to place multiple expressions in conversation with each other. Even the expressionless eel plays an integral role in emphasizing her keen sense of observation. By including a faceless eel and making it adjacent to an expressive cat and even more animated children, Leyster demarcated her adroitness at creating a hierarchy of expression. The poor eel is confined to the most basic gestures of body language.

In *Two Children with a Cat* and *Two Children with a Cat and an Eel*, the children's large smiles and the pet's emotional eyes equally validate Leyster's range as an artist capable of more than just portraits, for striking a balance between conveying heightened expression and maintaining a sense of freshness and purity was not readily palpable in other artists' works, as has been shown in this book. Ultimately, this sense of freshness and purity leads to another

---

[287] Ibid, 202.
[288] Ibid.
[289] Ibid.

similarity shared by both works, which is the preservation of innocence through the artist's ability to capture a range of spontaneous natural expression.

In the final analysis, this is something we found, too, in Leyster's *Self Portrait*. The children, no matter how wily their actions are towards the pets, remain mere children acting their ages. By the same token, Leyster, though an adult in her self-portrait, echoes the jubilation of the musician on her canvas and vice versa, therefore sustaining a quality of childlike innocence. By contributing to this quality via his expression, the musician becomes more than simply a supplementary component, just as the cats and eel are more than mere subsidiary elements by being incorporated into a hierarchy of expression. Beyond merely demonstrating a continuous spirit of innocence in Leyster's paintings of children and animals, this chapter has shown that even the blankest of faces, rudimentary of gestures, and smallest of figures could accomplish the conflation of separate painting genres, therefore contributing greatly to our understanding of Leyster's ingenuity.

Conclusion

Leyster's painting techniques may be regarded as having emerged from her historical, religious, and socio-political contexts, particularly the independent spirit of Dutch Protestantism. Her studio training in a predominantly male field, her blending of portraiture and genre scenes, and her inclusion of bright colors, costumes, direct gazes, and specific poses, however, all transcend the contexts within which she worked and point to her versatility, confidence, and display of adroitness. This self-assurance is discernable in the comparisons between Leyster's paintings and those of her male contemporaries. Whereas many of her male contemporaries demonstrated their skills through the inclusion of symbolic worldly objects situated before obscured canvases, Leyster proudly revealed herself in a brightly lit canvas while smiling open-mouthed and casually leaning back in her chair, both of which were bold, unconventional employments of expression and pose. Even the self-portraits by her female predecessors that utilized a similar composition (gazing out at the viewer while sitting proudly before an unveiled canvas) are not as daring as Leyster's, for they do not match the unexpected spontaneity of her expression and pose, nor her animated use of swift brushstrokes and inclusion of genre scene imagery. Leyster's paintings of children hone the same characteristics, therefore allowing her young subjects to waver not only between portraiture and genre scenes, but also between the depiction of childlike innocence and adult maturity. Finally, it is this childlike innocence that separates Leyster's paintings of children and animals from earlier and contemporary artists' paintings of children and animals. While other artists depicted children as miniature adults intended only to serve as vehicles through which to convey erotic and moral nuances (often at the animals' expenses under the guise of play), Leyster showcased both children and animals as worthy and valuable studies of expression.

This examination has sought to ask new questions about Leyster's imagery. Innumerable ones remain, however, about this under-appreciated artist, particularly since a second self-portrait (fig. 34) was discovered as recently as 2016.[290] Unlike the light, jovial self-portrait which has been the focus of this entire study, the newly-discovered one from 1653 shows Leyster standing before an empty, dark background.[291] Her easel is not observable, and the palette clutched in her hand seems to only contain one color.[292] This single color adheres to a dark color scheme consisting of subdued blacks, whites, and browns which, coupled with Leyster's upright posture and determined, downward gaze, communicate her seriousness to viewers.[293] Produced for her family rather than to be sold at market, the self-portrait attests to the solemnity of her talent, countless years of experience, and a life dedicated to painting.[294] Her collar, with its delicate lace details, signifies technical prowess and connotes that a lifelong devotion to painting has garnered her financial success.[295] For these reasons, the painting focuses all attention on Leyster and not on the process of art-making itself.[296]

With this recently-discovered work, fresh comparisons may be drawn between it and Leyster's previous self-portrait, as well as between it and other self-portraits by early modern male and female artists. A new chapter in the study of Leyster's life and career has commenced,

---

[290] Christie's experts discovered the work while appraising the contents of an English country estate whose owners were oblivious to the value of the painting that had hung in their home for centuries. The work was authenticated by Frima Fox Hofrichter and auctioned off by Christie's in 2016 for $593,883. On this, see Artnet News, "Long-Lost Self-Portrait by Dutch Master Judith Leyster Discovered in English Estate" https://news.artnet.com/art-world/self-portrait-dutch-master-judith-leyster-discovered-797885 (01-26-20)

[291] The Art Story, "Judith Leyster Artworks" https://www.theartstory.org/artist/leyster-judith/artworks/ (01-26-20)

[292] Ibid.

[293] Ibid.

[294] Artnet News, "Long-Lost Self-Portrait by Dutch Master Judith Leyster Discovered in English Estate" https://news.artnet.com/art-world/self-portrait-dutch-master-judith-leyster-discovered-797885 (01-26-20); The Art Story, "Judith Leyster Artworks" https://www.theartstory.org/artist/leyster-judith/artworks/ (01-26-20)

[295] The Art Story, "Judith Leyster Artworks" https://www.theartstory.org/artist/leyster-judith/artworks/ (01-26-20)

[296] Ibid.

and this examination of Leyster's unique applications of expression may be the gateway to that chapter.

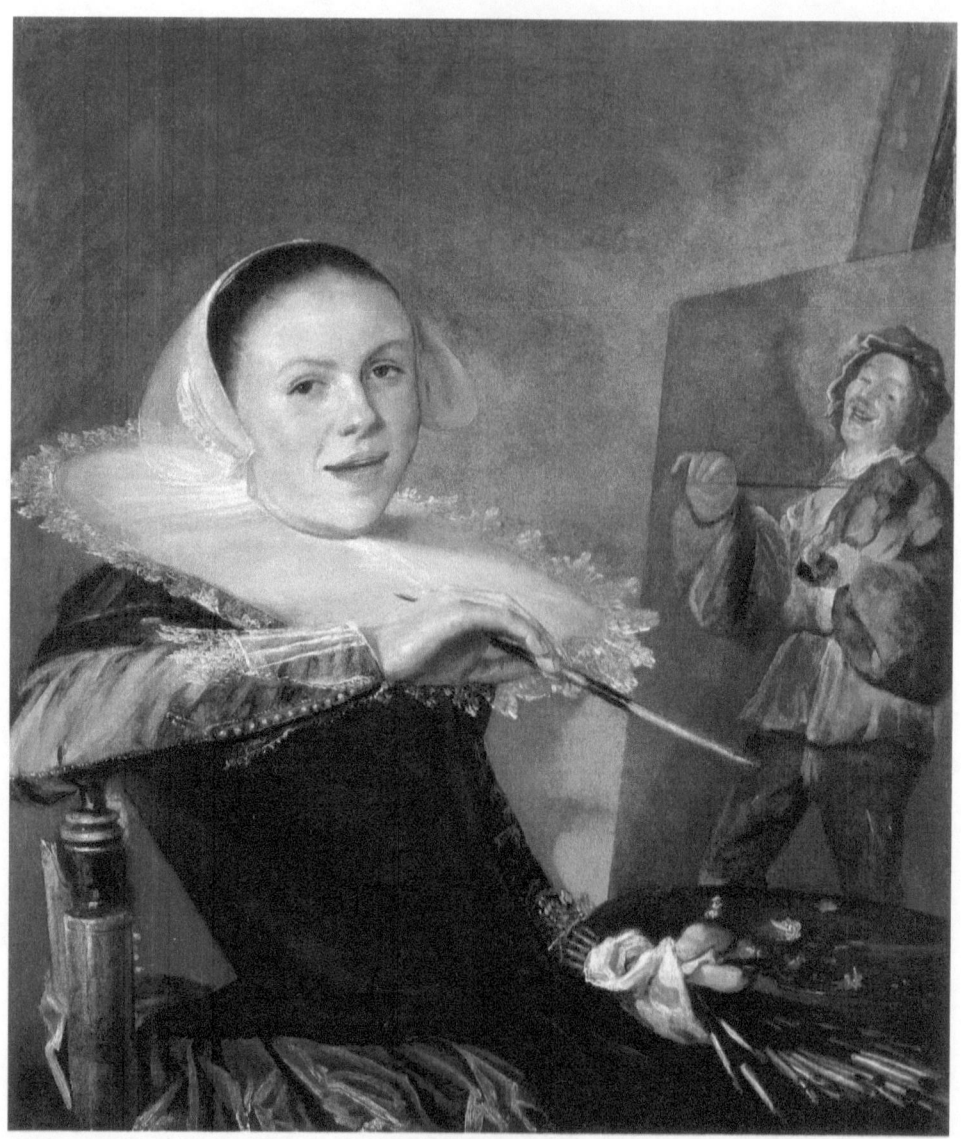

Fig. 1. Judith Leyster, *Self Portrait*, 1635, oil on canvas, 29 in. x 26 in., National Gallery of Art, Washington.

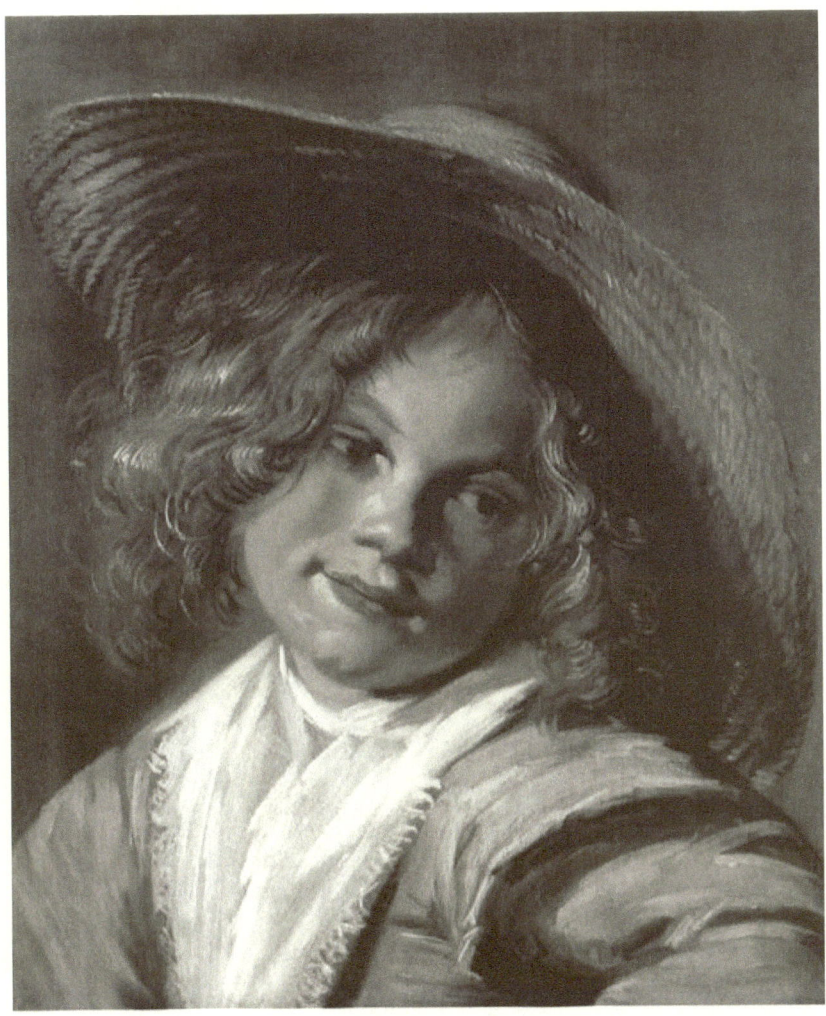

Fig. 2. Judith Leyster, *Girl with a Straw Hat*, 1635, oil on panel, 14 in. x 12 in., Foundation Rau pour le Tiers-Monde, Zurich.

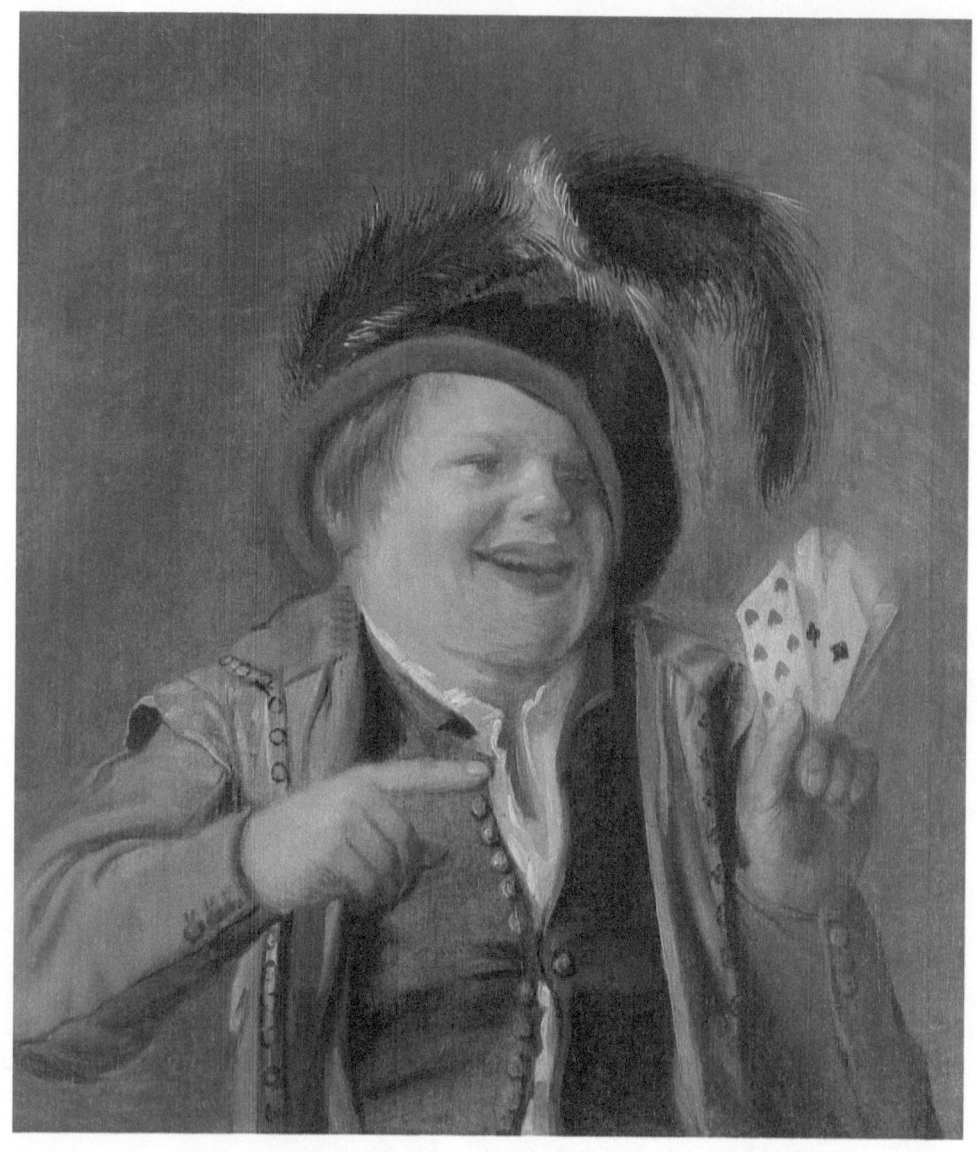

Fig. 3. Judith Leyster, *A Card Player*, 1630, oil on panel, 13.8 in. x 12.2 in., Private collection.

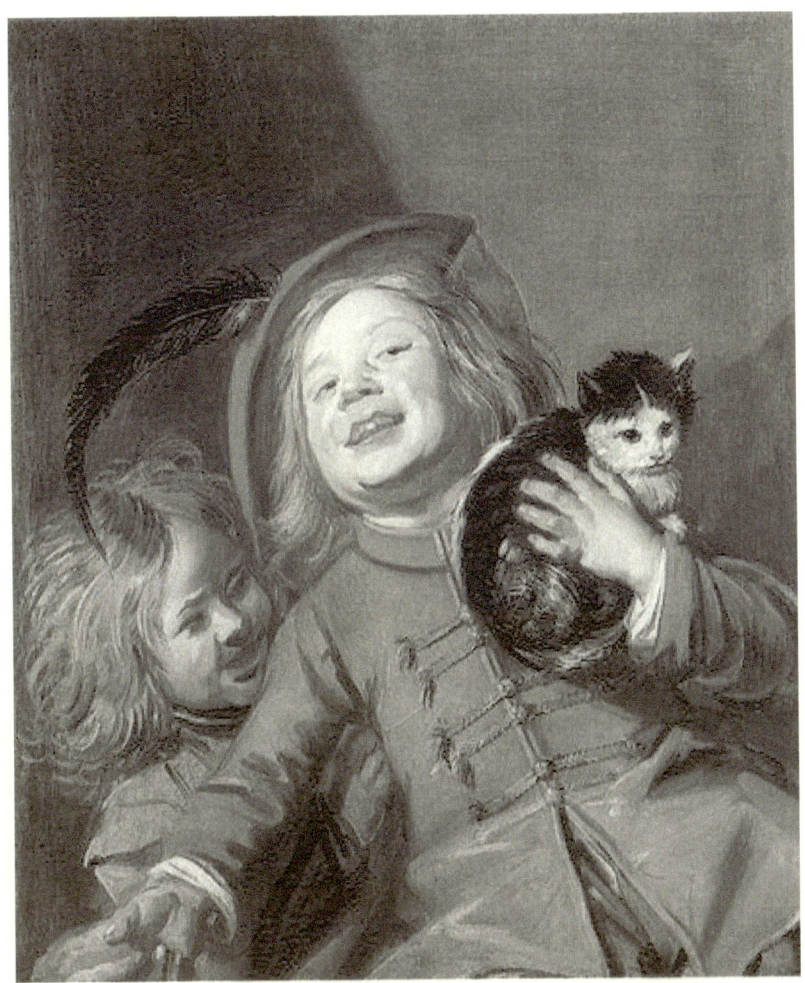

Fig. 4. Judith Leyster, *Two Children with a Cat*, 1629, oil on canvas, 24 in. x 20 in., Private collection.

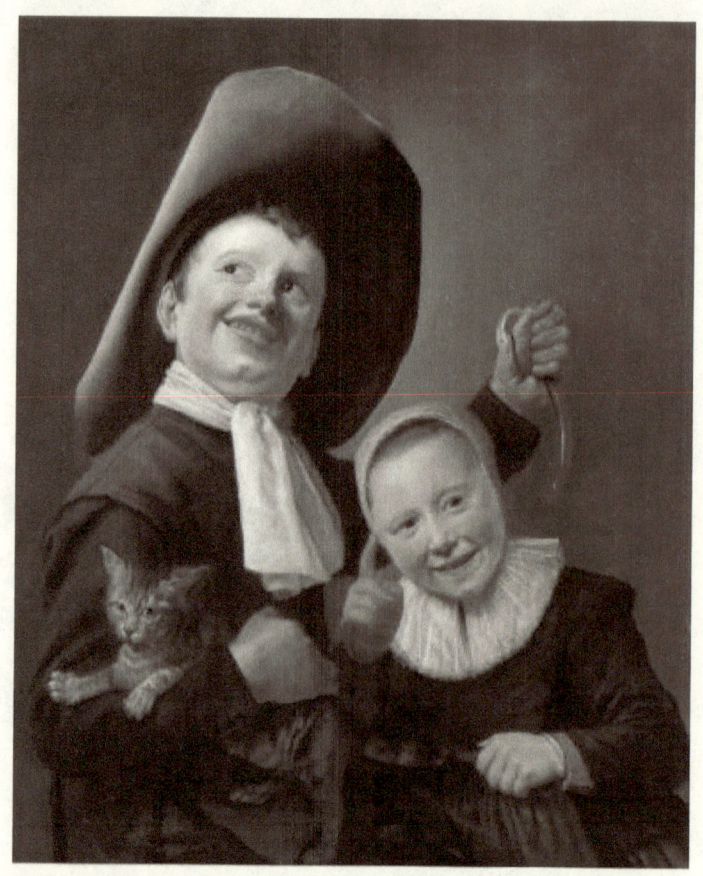

Fig. 5. Judith Leyster, *A Boy and a Girl with a Cat and an Eel*, 1630, oil on panel, 23 in. x 19 in.,
National Gallery, London.

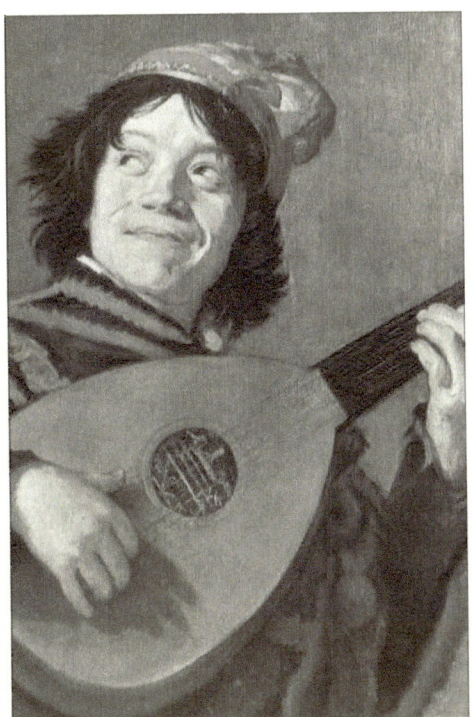

Fig. 6. Attributed to Judith Leyster, *The Jester*, 1625, oil on canvas, 26 in. x 23 in.,
Rijksmuseum, Amsterdam.

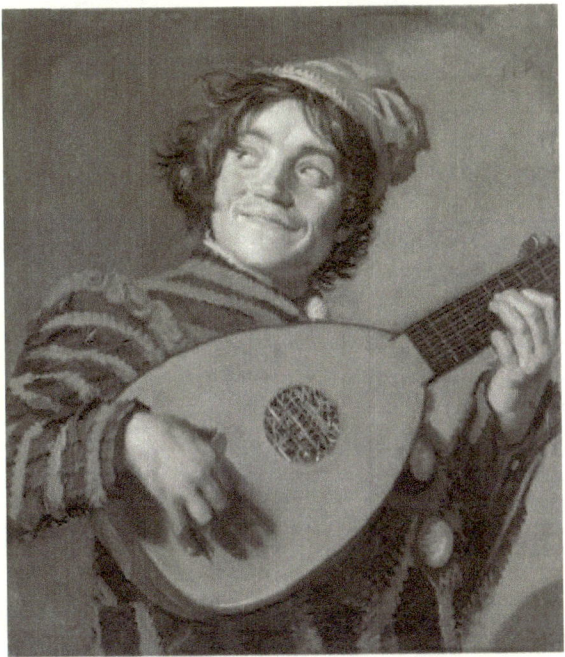

Fig. 7. Frans Hals, *Lute Player*, 1623, oil on canvas, 27 in. x 24 in., Louvre Museum, Paris.

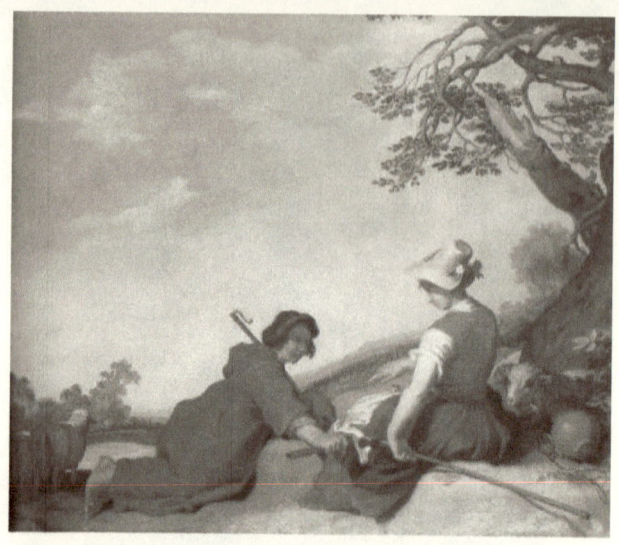

Fig. 8. Abraham Bloemaert, *Shepherd and Shepherdess*, 1627, oil on canvas.

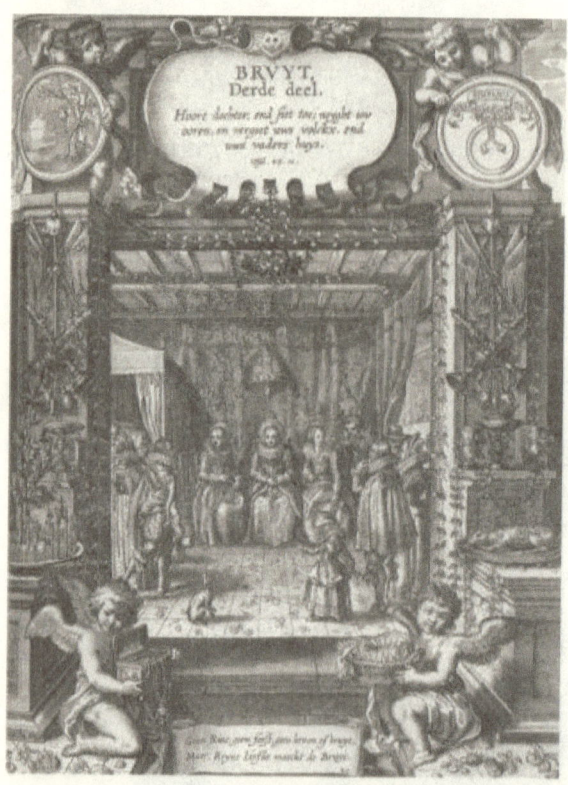

Fig. 9. Adriaen van de Veene, *Bride in Houwelick*, 17th century, etching, University of Amsterdam Library, Netherlands.

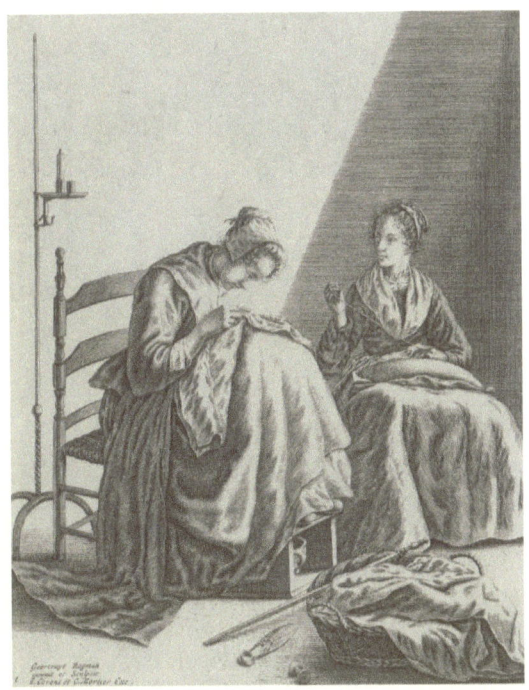

Fig. 10. Geertruyd Rogman, *Woman Sewing*, c. 1640-57, engraving, 8 in. x 6 ½ in., The Metropolitan Museum of Art, New York.

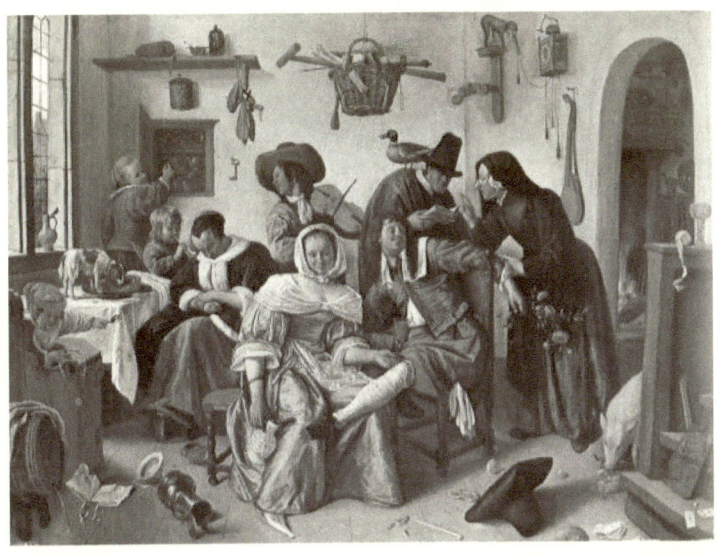

Fig. 11. Jan Steen, *In Luxury, Look Out*, 1663, oil on canvas, 40 in. x 57 in., Kunsthistorisches Museum, Vienna.

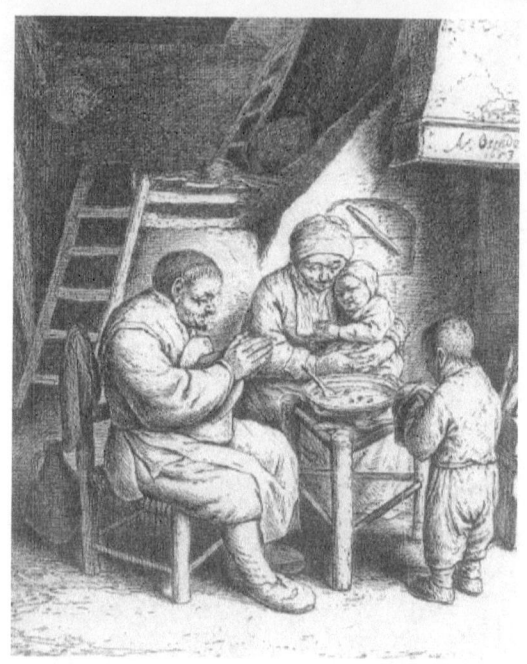

Fig. 12. Adriaen van Ostade, *Prayer Before the Meal*, 1653, etching, 6 in. x 5 in., British Museum, London.

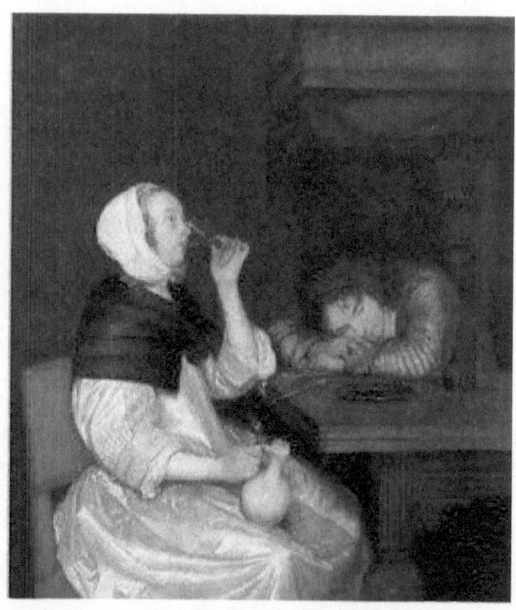

Fig. 13. Gerrit ter Borch, *Woman Drinking Wine with a Drunken Soldier*, 1658-59, oil on canvas, Private collection.

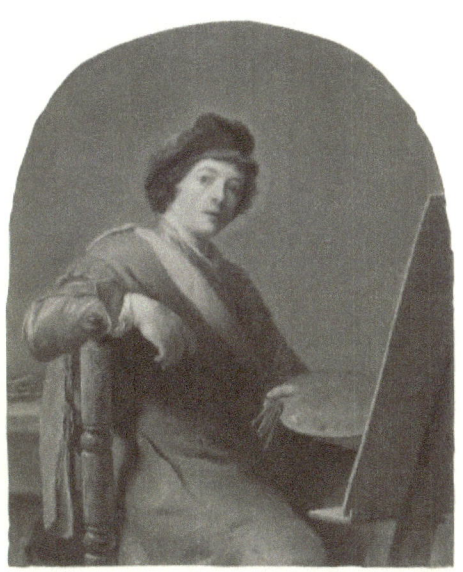

Fig. 14. Attributed to Cornelis Bisschop, *Self-Portrait of an Artist Seated at an Easel*, c. 1653, oil on panel, 11 in. x 9 in., The Leiden Collection.

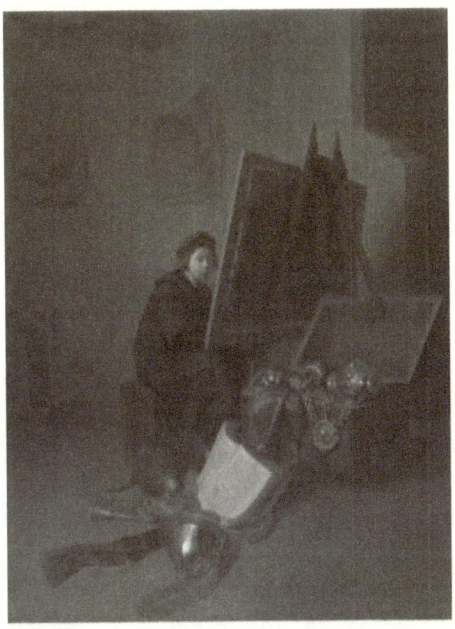

Fig. 15. Attributed to Gerrit Dou, *Self-Portrait (?) at an Easel*, c. 1628-29, oil on panel, 26 in. x 20 in., The Leiden Collection.

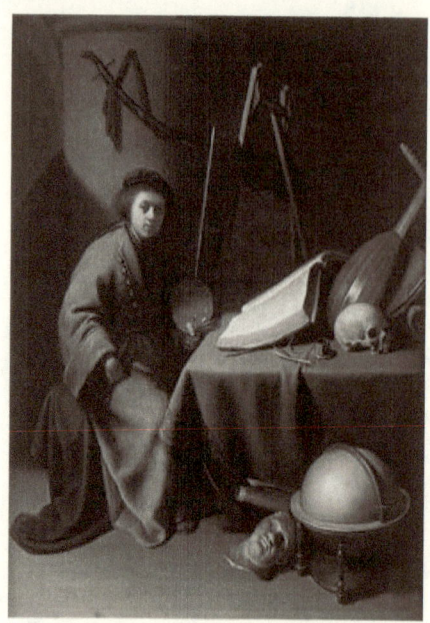

Fig. 16. Attributed to Gerrit Dou, *Artist at His Easel*, c. 1630-32, oil on panel, 23 ¼ in. x 17 1/8 in., Private collection.

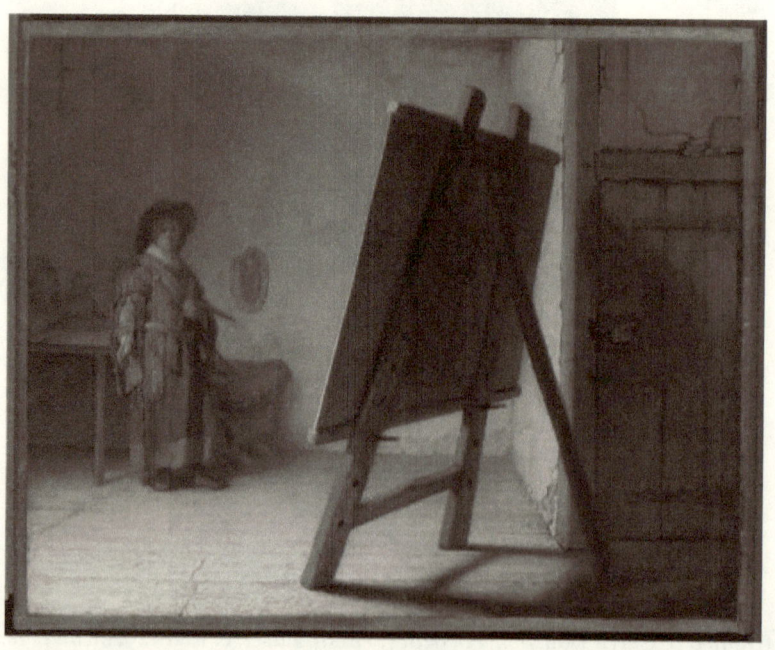

Fig. 17. Rembrandt, *Artist in his Studio*, 1628, oil on panel, Museum of Fine Arts, Boston.

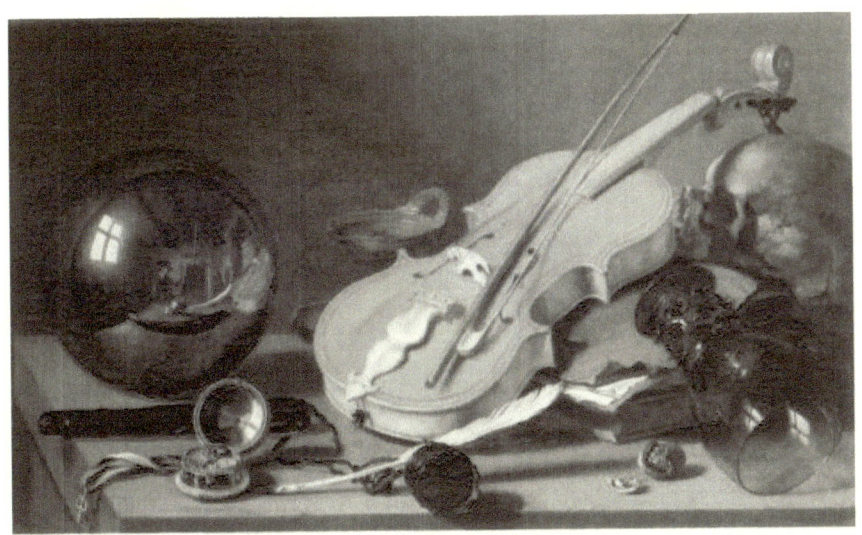

Fig. 18. Pieter Claesz, *Vanitas Still Life*, c. 1628, oil on panel, 14 in. x 23 ½ in., Germanisches
Nationalmuseum, Nuremberg.

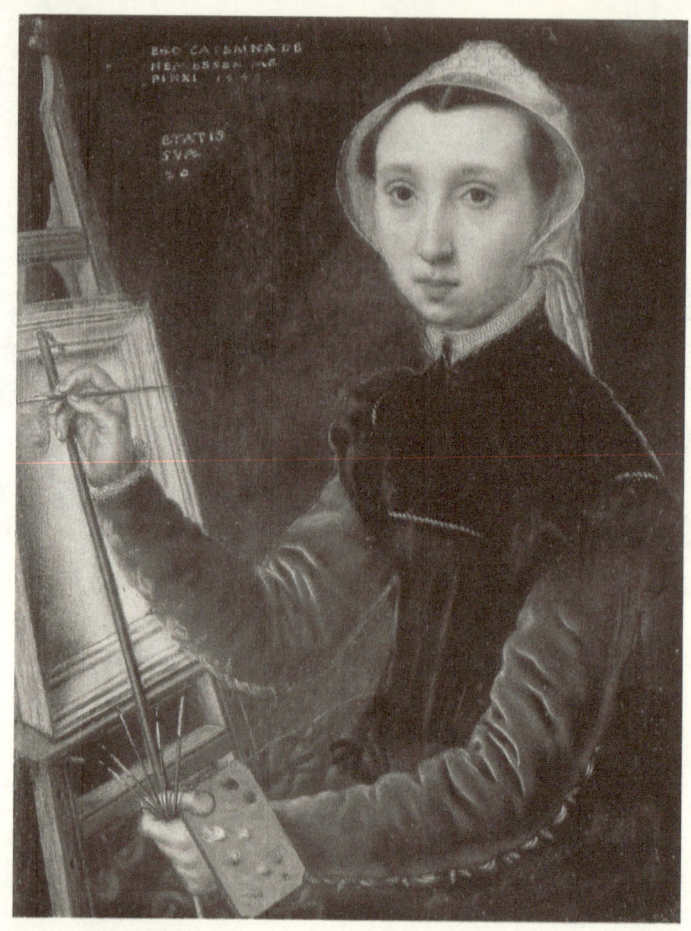

Fig. 19. Caterina van Hemessen, *Self Portrait*, 1548, oil on panel, 12 in. x 10 in., Öffentliche Kunstsammlungen, Kunstmuseum, Basel.

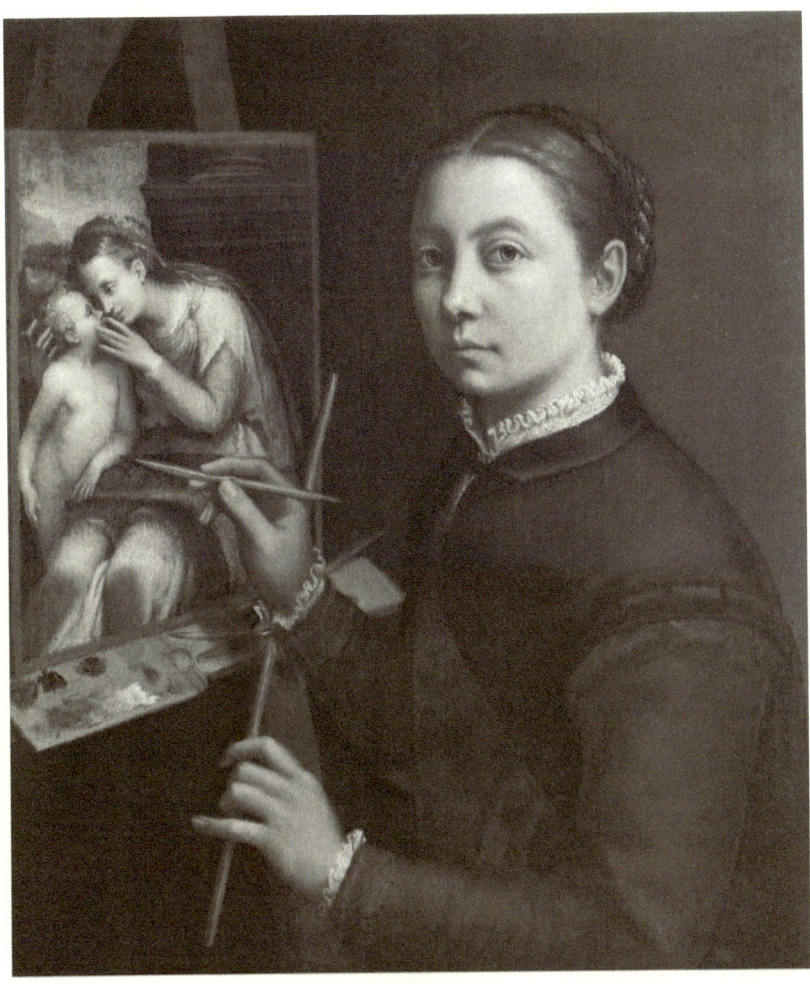

Fig. 20. Sofonisba Anguissola, *Self Portrait*, 1556, oil on canvas, 26 in. x 22 in., Lancut Museum, Poland.

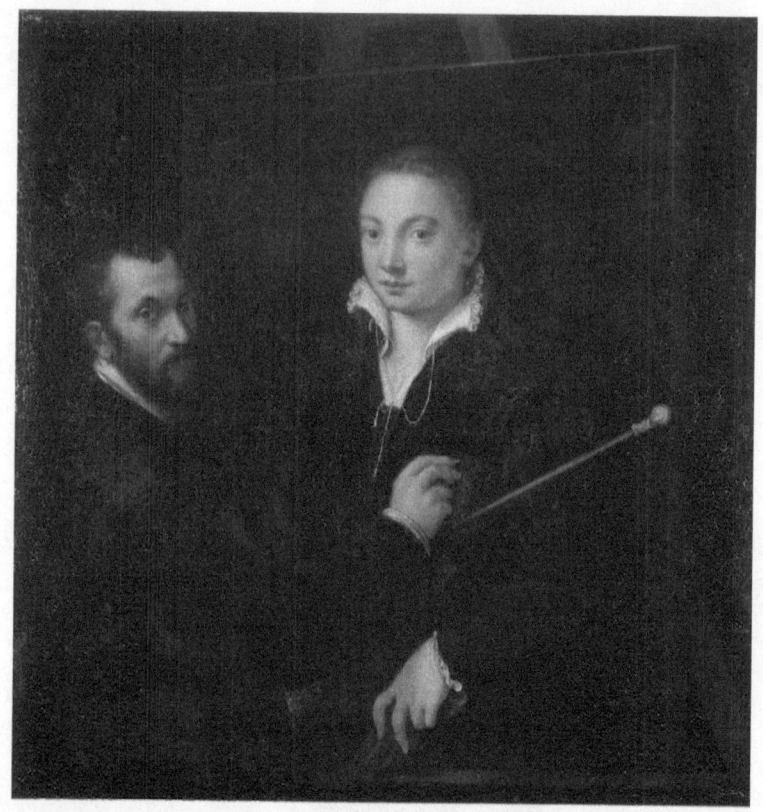

Fig. 21. Sofonisba Anguissola, *Self Portrait with Bernardino Campi*, 1559, oil on canvas, 43 in. x 39 in., Spannocchi Collection and Pinacoteca Nazionale di Siena, Italy.

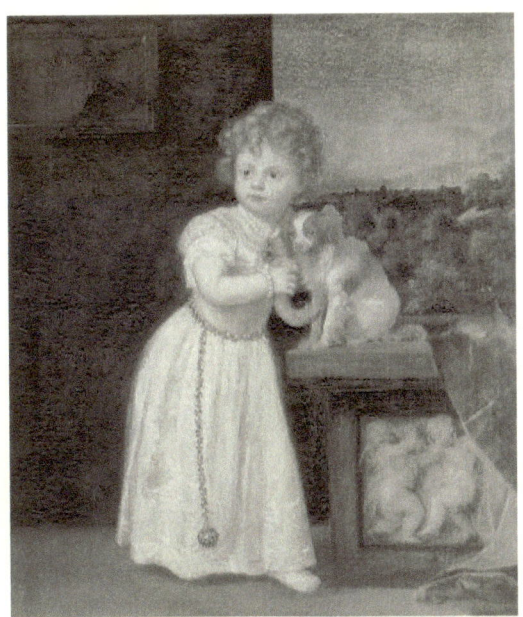

Fig. 22. Titian, *Portrait of Clarissa Strozzi*, 1542, oil on canvas, 45 in. x 38 in., Berlin State Museums, Berlin.

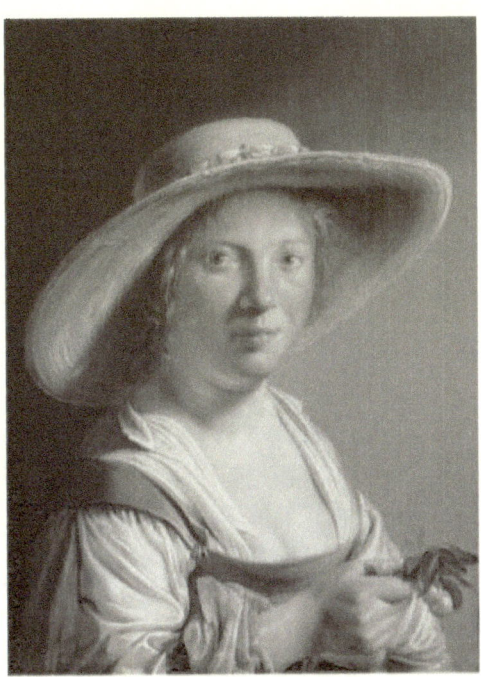

Fig. 23. Salomon de Bray, *Shepherdess*, 1635, oil on panel, 8 in. x 6 in., Formerly Robert Noortman Gallery, London.

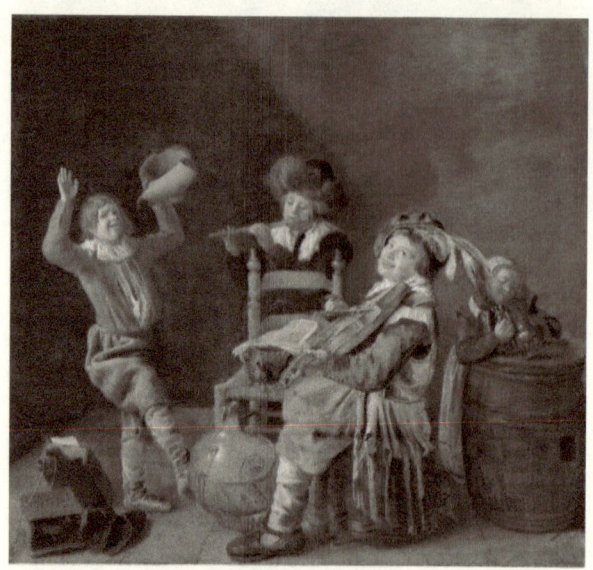

Fig. 24. Jan Miense Molenaer, *Children Making Music*, c. 1630s, oil on panel, 15.7 in. x 17.5 in., Wawel Castle, Krakow, Poland.

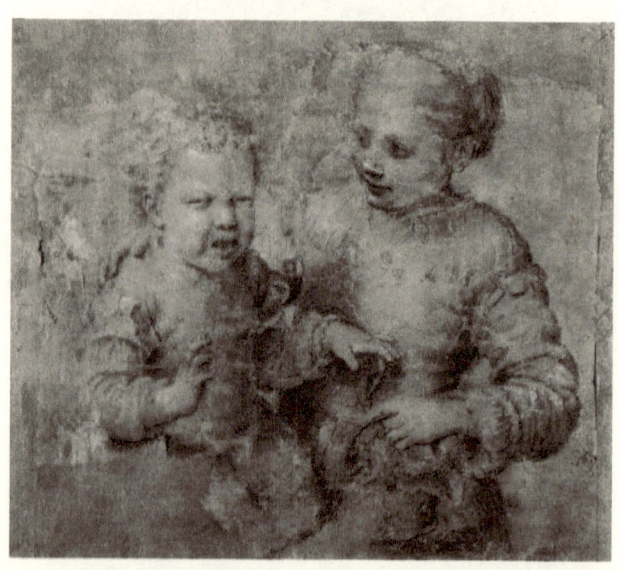

Fig. 25. Sofonisba Anguissola, *Boy Bitten by a Crawfish*, 1554, black chalk and charcoal on brown paper, 13 in. x 15 in., Museo Nazionale di Capodimonte, Naples.

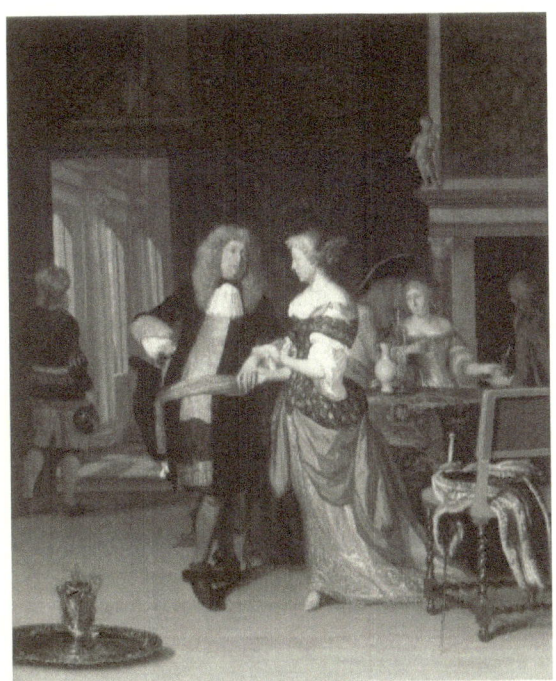

Fig. 26. Eglon Hendrik Van der Neer, *Couple in an Interior*, c. 1675, oil on canvas, 33.6 in. x 27.5 in., Private collection.

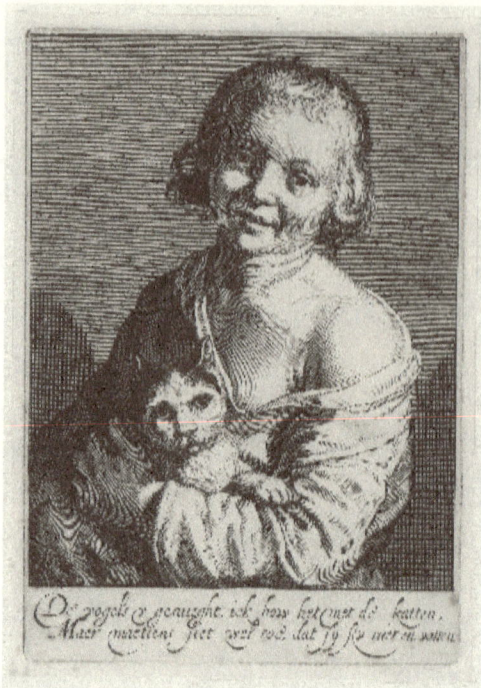

Fig. 27. Cornelis Bloemaert, *Child with a Cat*, 1625, engraving, 4 in. x 6 in., Museum of New Zealand, Wellington, New Zealand.

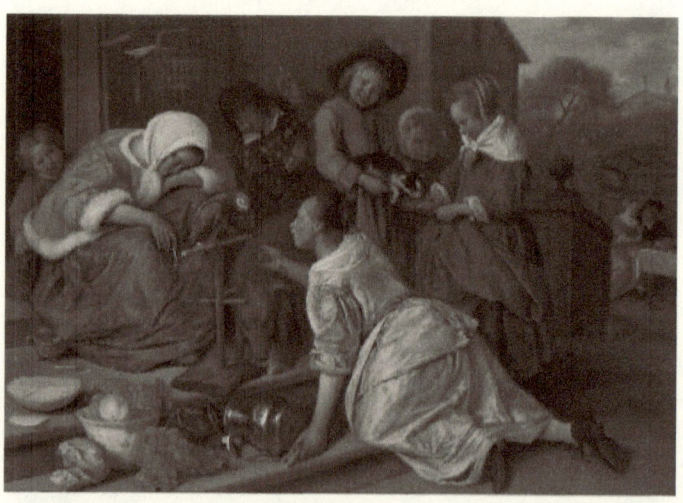

Fig. 28. Jan Steen, *The Effects of Intemperance*, 1663-65, oil on wood, 29 in. x 41 in., National Gallery, London.

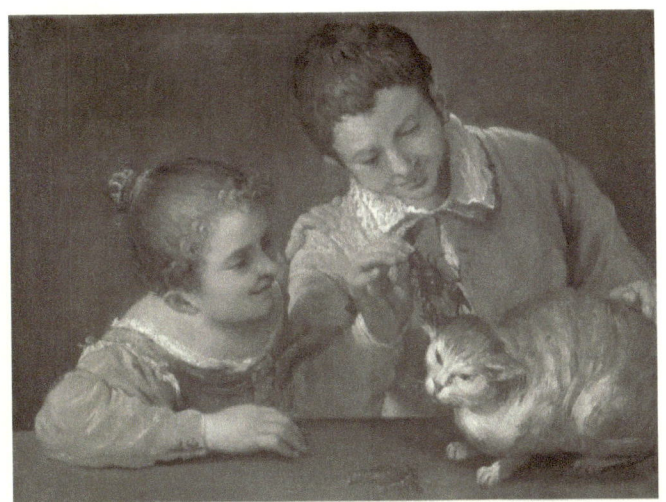

Fig. 29. Annibale Carracci, *Two Children Teasing a Cat*, 1590, oil on canvas, 26 in. x 35 in., The Metropolitan Museum of Art, New York.

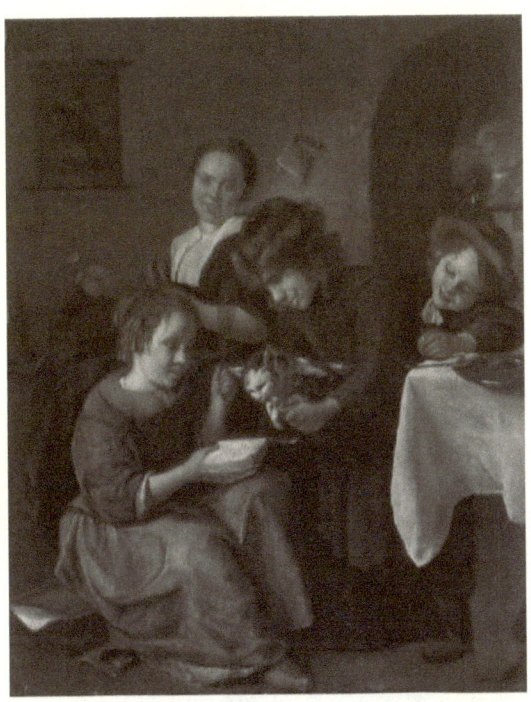

Fig. 30. Jan Steen, *Children Teaching a Cat to Read*, 1665-68, oil on panel, 17.7 in. x 13.9 in., Kunstmuseum Basel, Switzerland.

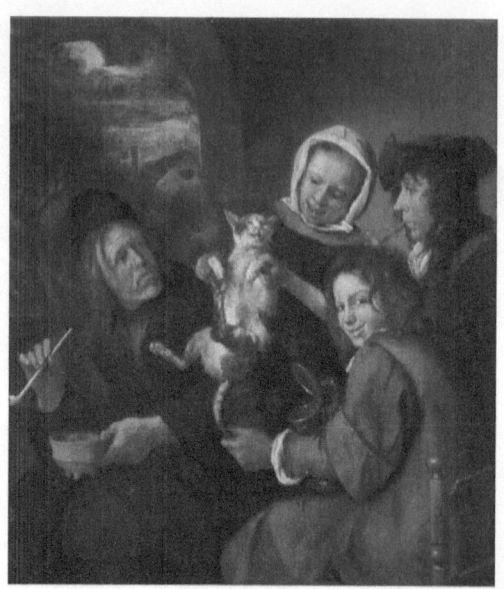

Fig. 31. Jan Steen, *Children Teasing a Cat*, 1665, oil on panel, 16 in. x 14 in., Private collection, Kanne, Belgium.

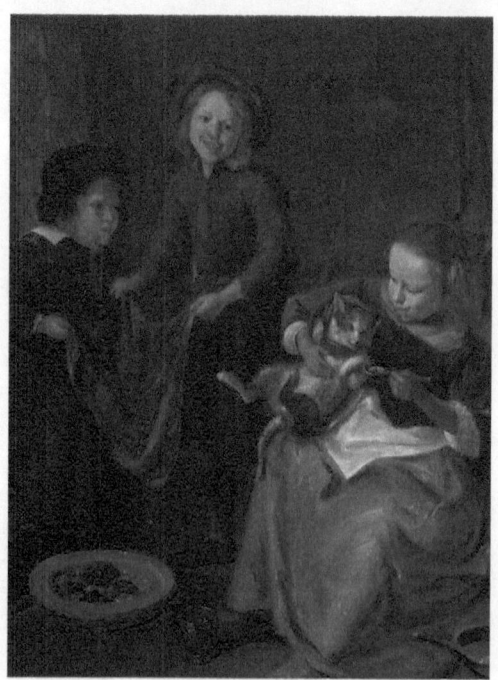

Fig. 32. Jan Steen, *The Cat's Medicine*, 1663, oil on panel, 22 in. x 18 in., San Diego Museum of Art, California.

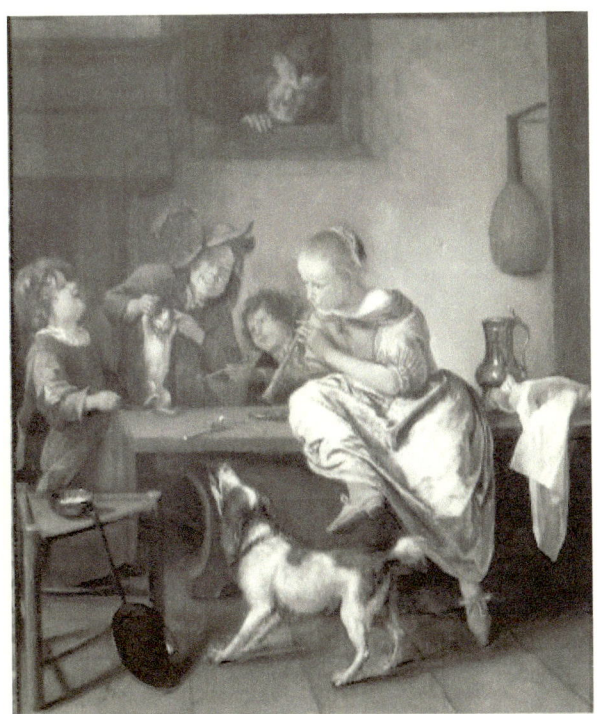

Fig. 33. Jan Steen, *Children Teaching a Cat to Dance*, 1660-79, oil on panel, 26 in. x 23 in., Rijksmuseum, Amsterdam.

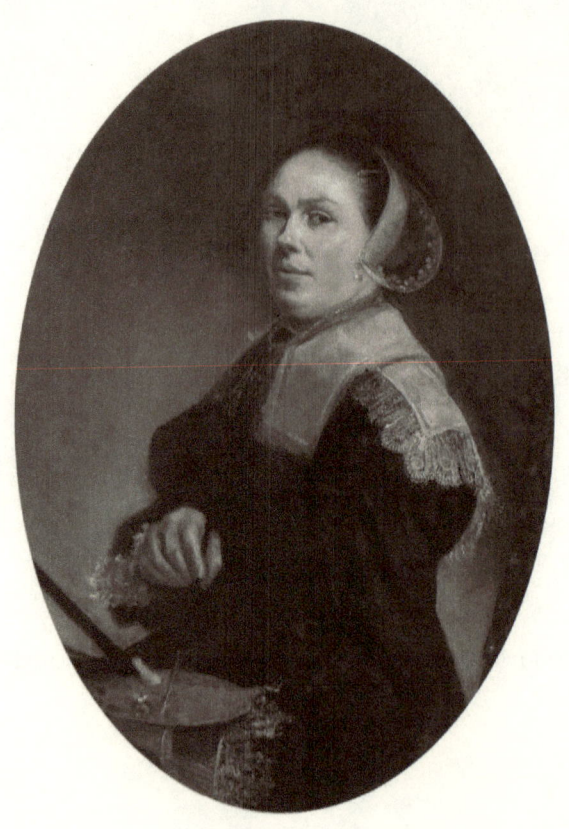

Fig. 34. Judith Leyster, *Self Portrait*, 1653, oil on canvas, 12.1 in. x 8.6 in., Private collection.

Bibliography

Artnet News, "Long-Lost Self-Portrait by Dutch Master Judith Leyster Discovered in English
Estate" https://news.artnet.com/art-world/self-portrait-dutch-master-judith-leyster-
discovered-797885 (01-26-20)

Barasch, Mosche. *Modern Theories of Art 2: From Impressionism to Kandinsky*. New York:
NYU Press, 1998.

Barolsky, Paul and Lawrence Goedde. "Ambiguity in Rembrandt's Boston *Artist in His
Studio*," *Notes in the History of Art* 30 (Summer 2011): 43-45.

Bass, Laura R. *The Drama of the Portrait: Theater and Visual Culture in Early Modern Spain*.
University Park: Penn State University Press, 2009.

Biesboer, Pieter. *Collections of Paintings in Haarlem 1572-1745*. Los Angeles: J. Paul Getty
Museum, 2002.

Biesboer, Pieter, Martina Brunner-Bulst, et al. *Pieter Claesz: Master of Haarlem Still Life*.
Haarlem: Frans Hals Museum, 2004.

Boers, M.E.W. "Pieter De Molijn (1597-1661): A Dutch Painter and the Art Market in the
Seventeenth Century," *Journal of Historians of Netherlandish Art* (2017): 1-25.

Brilliant, Richard. *Portraiture*. London: Reaktion Books, 2004.

Castiglione, Baldassare. *The Book of the Courtier*. Translated by Leonard Eckstein Opdycke.
New York: Charles Scribner's Sons, 1901.

Chadwick, Whitney. *Women, Art and Society*. London: Thames & Hudson, 1990.

Davies, David William. *A Primer of Dutch Seventeenth Century Overseas Trade*. Heidelberg,
Germany: Springer Netherlands, 2013.

De Groot, Cornelis Hofstede. "Judith Leyster. Mit einer Lichtdrucktafel und zwei Abbildungen

im Text," *Jahrbuch der Königlich Preussischen Kunstsammlungen* 14 (1893): 190-198,
232.

De Marchi, Neil and Hans J. Van Miegroet. *Mapping Markets for Paintings in Europe, 1450-
1750*. Turnhout, Belgium: Brepols Publishers, 2006).

Dekker, Rudolf Michel. "Women in the Medieval and Early Modern Netherlands," *Journal of
Women's History* 10.2 (1998): 165-88.

Descartes, René. *Discourse on the Method of Rightly Conducting One's Reason and of Seeking
Truth in the Sciences*. Leiden: René Descartes, 1637.

Dreyfus, Hubert and Mark A. Wrathall. *A Companion to Phenomenology and Existentialism*.
Hoboken, NJ: Wiley, 2009.

Felix-Jäger, Steven and Amos Yong. *Pentecostal Aesthetics: Theological Reflections in a
Pentecostal Philosophy of Art and Aesthetics*. Boston: Brill Academic Publishers, 2015.

Fox Hofrichter, Frima. *Judith Leyster, 1609–1660*. Washington, DC: National Gallery of Art,
2009.

Fox Hofrichter, Frima. *Judith Leyster: A Woman Painter in Holland's Golden Age*.
Doornspijk, Netherlands: Davaco Publishers, 1989.

Franits, Wayne E. *Dutch Seventeenth-Century Genre Painting: Its Stylistic and Thematic
Evolution*. New Haven and London: Yale University Press, 2004.

Franits, Wayne E. *From Revolt to Riches: Culture and History of the Low Countries, 1500–
1700*. United Kingdom: UCL Press, 2017.

Freedman, Luba. "Titian's *Portrait of Clarissa Strozzi*: The State Portrait of a Child," *Jahrbuch
der Berliner Museen* 31 (1989): 165-180.

Garrard, Mary. "Here's Looking at Me: Sofonisba Anguissola and the Problem of the Woman
Artist," *Renaissance Quarterly* 47 (1994): 556.

Goodyear, William Henry. *Renaissance and Modern Art*. New York: Flood & Vincent, 1894.

Grootenboer, Hanneke. "How to Become a Picture: Theatricality as Strategy in Seventeenth-

Century Dutch Portraits," *Art History* 33 (2010): 320-333.

Harbison, Craig. *The Mirror of the Artist: Northern Renaissance Art in its Historical Context.*

    Upper Saddle River, NJ: Laurence King Publishing Limited, 1995.

Harms, Juliane. "Judith Leyster, ihr Leben und ihr Werk," *Oud-Holland* 44 (1927).

Heller, Nancy G. *Women Artists: An Illustrated History.* New York: Abbeville Press, 1997.

Hoenselaars, Ton and Rui Carvalho Homem. *Translating Shakespeare for the Twenty-First*

    Century. Amsterdam, Netherlands: Rodopi, 2004.

Honig, Elizabeth Alice. "Desire and Domestic Economy," *The Art Bulletin* 83 (2001): 294-315.

Honig, Elizabeth Alice. "The Art of Being 'Artistic': Dutch Women's Creative

    Practices in the 17th Century," *Woman's Art Journal* 22 (2001-2002): 31-39.

Honig Fine, Elsa. "One Point Perspective," *Woman's Art Journal* 16 (1995-1996): 2.

Houbraken, Arnold. *De groote schouburgh der Nederlantsche konstschilders en schilderessen.*

    Digital Library for Dutch Literature, 1718.

Hutton, Deborah, and Rebecca Tucker. "The Worldly Artist in the Seventeenth Century: The

    Travels of Cornelis Claesz. Heda," *Art History* 37.5 (2014): 860-89.

Institute for Art Historical Research. *Artibus et Historiae: An Art Anthology.* Cracow, Poland:

    IRSA, 2008.

Israel, Jonathan. *The Dutch Republic: Its Rise, Greatness, and Fall, 1477–1806.* Oxford:

    Clarendon Press, 1995.

Jacobs, Fredrika H. "Woman's Capacity to Create: The Unusual Case of Sofonisba Anguissola,"

    Renaissance Quarterly 47 (1994): 74-101.

Jones, Susan Frances. *Van Eyck to Gossaert.* London: National Gallery, 2011.

Klein, Sheri. *Art and Laughter.* London: I.B. Tauris, 2006.

Loh, Maria. *Titian's Touch: Art, Magic and Philosophy.* United Kingdom: Reaktion Books,

    2019.

Maan, Tony. "Material Culture and Popular Calvinist Worldliness in the Dutch 'Golden Age,'"

History Compass 9 (2011): 284-299.

MacLaren, Neil and Christopher Brown. *Catalogue of the Dutch School, Vol. 2, 1600-1900.* Washington, D.C.: National Gallery, 1991.

Mérot, Alain. *French Painting in the Seventeenth Century.* New Haven: Yale University Press, 1995.

Moffitt Peacock, Martha. "Geertruydt Roghman and the Female Perspective in 17th-Century Dutch Genre Imagery," *Woman's Art Journal* 14 (Autumn, 1993 - Winter, 1994): 3-10.

Montagu, Jennifer. *The Expression of the Passions: The Origin and Influence of Charles Le Brun's Conference sur l'expression generale et particuliere.* New Haven and London: Yale University Press, 1994.

Murphy, Caroline P. *Lavinia Fontana: A Painter and her Patrons in Sixteenth-century Bologna.* New Haven and London: Yale University Press, 2003.

National Museum of Women in the Arts. *Women Artists of the Dutch Golden Age.* Washington, D.C.: National Museum of Women in the Arts, 2019. Exhibition pamphlet.

Nochlin, Linda. "Why Have There Been No Great Women Artists?" from *Art and Sexual Politics.* London: Collier Macmillan, 1973.

Orenstein, Nadine M. "Stepping Up to the Plate: The State of Research in Seventeenth-Century Dutch Prints" in Wayne E. Franits' *The Ashgate Companion to Dutch Painting.* London and New York: Routledge, 2016.

Perry, Gillian and Colin Cunningham. *Academies, Museums, and Canons of Art.* New Haven: Yale University Press, 1999.

Prak, Maarten Roy. *Craft Guilds in the Early Modern Low Countries: Work, Power and Representation.* Farnham, UK: Ashgate Publishing, 2006.

Prak, Maarten Roy. *The Dutch Republic in the Seventeenth Century: The Golden Age.* Cambridge, UK: Cambridge University Press, 2005.

Rasterhoff, Claartje. "Economic Aspects of Dutch Art" in Wayne E. Franits' *The Ashgate*

Research Companion to Dutch Art of the Seventeenth Century. London and New York: Routledge, 2016.

Reed, Laurel. "Art, Life, Charm, and Titian's Portrait of Clarissa Strozzi" in Albrecht Classen, *Childhood in the Middle Ages and the Renaissance: The Results of a Paradigm Shift in the History of* Mentality. Berlin: De Gruyter, 2005.

Rosenberg, Jakob, et al. *The Pelican History of Art: Dutch Art and Architecture 1600-1800*. Baltimore, Maryland: Penguin Books Inc., 1972.

Ruff, Alan R. *Arcadian Visions: Pastoral Influences on Poetry, Painting and the Design of Landscape*. Oxford, UK: Windgather Press, 2015.

Ruiz Gómez, Leticia. *A Tale of Two Women Painters: Sofonisba Anguissola and Lavinia Fontana*. Madrid: Museo Nacional del Prado, 2019.

Schama, Simon. "Wives and Wantons: Versions of Womanhood in 17th Century Dutch Art," *The Oxford Art Journal* 3 (1980): 5-13.

Schneider, Norbert. *Still Life*. Cologne: Taschen, 2003.

Shipp, Horace. *The Dutch Masters*. New York: Philosophical Library, Inc., 1953.

Skelly, Julia. *The Uses of Excess in Visual and Material Culture, 1600-2010*. Philadelphia: Taylor & Francis, 2014.

Smith, David R. "Irony and Civility: Notes on the Convergence of Genre and Portraiture in Seventeenth-Century Dutch Painting," *The Art Bulletin* 69 (September 1987): 407-424.

Spinks, Jennifer and Susan Broomhall. *Early Modern Women in the Low Countries: Feminizing Sources and Interpretations of the Past*. Farnham, UK: Ashgate Publishing, 2011.

Steel, Brian D. "Titian's Clarissa Strozzi: The Infant as Ideal Bride" in Matthew Knox Averett's *The Early Modern Child in Art and History*. Philadelphia: Taylor & Francis, 2015.

Stone-Ferrier, Linda. "An Assessment of Recent Scholarship on Seventeenth-Century Dutch

Genre Imagery" in Wayne E. Franits' *The Ashgate Research Companion to Dutch Art of the Seventeenth Century*. New York: Routledge, 2016.

Sutherland Harris, Ann. *Seventeenth-Century Art & Architecture*. Upper Saddle River, NJ: Pearson Education, Inc., 2005.

Sutherland Harris, Ann and Linda Nochlin. *Women Artists: 1550-1950*. Los Angeles: Museum Associates of the Los Angeles County Museum of Art, 1976.

The Art Story, "Judith Leyster Artworks" https://www.theartstory.org/artist/leyster-judith/artworks/ (01-26-20)

The New York Times, "A Dutch Golden Age? That's Only Half the Story" https://www.nytimes.com/2019/10/25/arts/design/dutch-golden-age-and-colonialism.html (2-9-20)

Tilghman, Benjamin. *Reflections on Aesthetic Judgment and Other Essays*. Farnham, UK: Ashgate Publishing, 2006.

Todorovic, Jelena. *The Spaces That Never Were in Early Modern Art: An Exploration of Edges and Frontiers*. Cambridge, UK: Cambridge Scholars Publishing, 2019.

University of Maryland. *Early Modern Women*. College Park, Maryland: Center for Renaissance & Baroque Studies, University of Maryland, 2010.

van Elk, Martine. *Early Modern Women's Writing: Domesticity, Privacy, and the Public Sphere in England and the Dutch Republic*. New York: Springer International Publishing, 2017.

van Emden, Frieda. "Judith Leyster, a Female Frans Hals," *The Art World* 3 (March 1918): 501.

Vasari, Giorgio. *The Lives of the Artists*. New York: Oxford University Press, 2008.

Venema, Janny. *Kiliaen van Rensselaer (1586-1643): Designing a New World*. Albany, NY: SUNY Press, 2011.

Wallis, Patrick. *Apprenticeship in Early Modern Europe*. Cambridge, UK: Cambridge University Press, 2019.

Weller, Dennis P. *Jan Miense Molenaer: Painter of the Dutch Golden Age*. Manchester, VT:

Hudson Hills, 2002.

Welu, James A. and Pieter Biesboer. *Judith Leyster: A Dutch Master and Her World*.

Worcester: Waanders Printers, Zwolle, 1993.

Westermann, Mariet. *A Worldly Art: The Dutch Republic, 1585-1718*. New York: Harry N.

Abrams, Incorporated, 1996.

Westermann, Mariet. *Rembrandt*. London: Phaidon Press, 2000.

Woods-Marsden, Joanna. *Renaissance Self-Portraiture*. New Haven and London: Yale

University Press, 1998.

Worcester Art Museum, *Judith Leyster: A Dutch Master and Her World* (Worcester,

Massachusetts: Worcester Art Museum, 1993). Exhibition pamphlet.